MEAN Girls

101½ Creative Strategies and Activities for Working with Relational Aggression

youth light
inc.

© 2008, 2007 by YouthLight, Inc.
Chapin, SC 29036

Cover Design and Layout by Diane Florence
Project Editing by Susan Bowman

ISBN: 1-59850-022-8
EAN: 978-1-59850-022-6

Library of Congress Number
2006937664

10 9 8 7 6 5 4 3
Printed in the United States

Dedications

FROM ALLYSON

To my wonderful husband Eric for his patience during the long hours, support through the new adventures and for always being my cheerleader and encourager. I am who I am today because of you and the unending gifts you give me everyday.

To my sunshine Asher, you remind me to be happy and feel blessed. Thank you for trying to understand why Mommy "was always on the computer."

To my Mom for your wisdom and guidance and for maintaining your sanity: not just while you raised me but for the months your dining room table was destroyed as I worked on this book. There really aren't words for how grateful I feel for the gifts you have given me on this journey of life.

To my sister Nicole, I am so thankful God put our lives together so I wouldn't have to go searching for my very best "heart" friend. It is wonderful to have someone you trust to share all your secrets with and know they are safe. Thank you for always listening and responding honestly.

To my sister Michelle (1967-1991), because of you I Believe.....You taught more in your brief and beautiful years on how to love and give back...Thank you for helping to shape who I am.

To Kaye...WOW! I am so thankful God saw us and said "...those two girls would make great business partners but even better friends!" What a "Turning Point" in our lives to get to share all this together! Nothing is work when we're together..."It is what it is!"

To my precious Lord for the doors He has opened and the opportunities He blesses me with. Without His umbrella of protection and perfect blue print for my life nothing would possible.

FROM KAYE

To my amazing daughter Brianna. You are my biggest cheerleader! Thank you for having the courage to always have a loving heart.

To my mom and dad...thanks for giving me the self-confidence and courage to follow where God is leading me. I love you. Dad–I miss you so much.

To my sisters, Cia and Patti, and my brother Trey...all of you have given me your unconditional love all of my life. I have loved being "the baby" of the family. Thank you for always showing me what true loving relationships are all about.

To Allyson–my business partner and best friend–we know what women can really accomplish when there is unconditional love and support. Thank you for always providing the safety to be who God created me to be. "It is what it is!"

Most importantly, to God and His Son Jesus–for teaching me what relationships are truly supposed to be. I am nothing without you.

Acknowledgements

We would like to thank those women who have been pioneers in the field of female relationships. Thank you for your hard work and dedication. We hope to contribute to the solidarity of women as you have.

Thank you to Bob and Susan Bowman for their patience, guidance and friendship throughout this process. We have been blessed to be a part of this journey. Thank you for the opportunity!

A very special thank you to Patti Long. Thank you for "English Professor" eye.

Thank you to Diane Florence for your talents that make this book come alive. Thanks also for your patience as we edit and edit and edit!

Most importantly, we would like to thank God for His direction, guidance and humor. We know that we are well loved by Him!

Table of Contents

How to use this book 5

Introduction 6

Understanding Relational Aggression 7

Forms of Relational Aggression 7

Methods of Relational Aggression 8

Cyber-Bullying 9

Statistics 15

Short and Long Term Effects of Relational Aggression......................16

Misguided Interventions in Approaching Relational Aggression 17

101 1/2 Creative Strategies and Activities

(Strategies 1-4) Assessing Who's Who: Tools You Can Use...................18

(Strategies 5-35) Individual Interventions 32

(Strategies 36-53) Classroom or Small Group Activities 71

(Strategies 54-80) School Interventions 98

(Strategies 81-99) Parent Interventions 114

(Strategies 100-101 1/2) Wrap it Up!! 124

References 127

About the Authors 128

How to Use This Book

This book is intended to be used by the helping professional who has encountered a child or adolescent affected by relational aggression (RA). We have included many different approaches that we believe can be effective in reaching and helping young people.

The strategies and activities in this book can be used with an individual child or adolescent (C/A) or in a small group setting. These activities are intended to help children or adolescents (C/A's) explore and share their feelings and increase their understanding of the harmful effects of RA. This can help you connect with the C/A's and understand their thoughts and emotions while helping them to explore various ways of combating RA. You will find that many of these strategies and activities can be used for both boys and girls.

We have designed this book for the professional and the child/adolescent. Some of the strategies are for you, the professional, to utilize in the setting of your school or facility. Other strategies are designed for the C/A to use and accept the challenge to combat relational aggression. Many of the strategies include reproducible worksheets or may be completed on a separate sheet of paper.

These strategies have been successfully used in private practice and in school settings with various populations. We hope you will take the time to explore the strategies and activities in this book and consider adding them to your repertoire when working with children and adolescents.

Using a variety of creative approaches you can help children/adolescents learn to make meaningful connections. Our desire is for our children to incorporate what they have learned and teach their sisters, friends, and one day their daughters these invaluable life lessons.

In addition, this book is designed to help implement school-wide reform in addressing relational aggression. We have included many ideas and strategies to help you succeed in creating positive and lasting changes in your schools.

Introduction

Mean Girls...they are in every school and at all grade levels including preschool and kindergarten (Nelson et al, 2005). RA begins in preschool, peaks in middle and persists in high school. Rosalind Wiseman's book, *Queen Bees and Wannabees* increased awareness in our society of relational aggression among our girls, and with the popularity of the movie, "Mean Girls," we were exposed to the pain and suffering felt by children and adolescents touched by Relational Aggression today.

Just what is Relational Aggression and why is it important? Nicki Crick, a professor at the University of Minnesota and the director of the Institute of Child Development, pioneered studies identifying RA in girls. For more than a decade, Crick has conducted longitudinal studies of relational aggression, seen mainly in girls. Relational aggression is a form of bullying. RA is a form of emotional and psychological violence and can negatively effect the social and psychological adjustment of our youth. Crick's research has identified RA as intentional harm inflicted through the manipulation and destruction of peer relationships. Her research further identified that RA can take on different forms such as: malicious gossip, spreading rumors, lies, telling secrets, social exclusion, cyber bullying, and threats to withdraw friendships (Crick et al., 1996).

Trudy Ludwig, author of *My Secret Bully*, states that RA is putting conditions on a friendship, and it starts early. You've heard of conditional love; this is conditional friendship. Given that this behavior does begin early, addressing the problem of RA as soon as possible is vitally important, both at home and in the schools.

Understanding Relational Aggression

VARIOUS FORMS OF RELATIONAL AGGRESSION

Relational Aggression is complex and subtle. The following are various forms of Relational Aggression as defined by the Ophelia Project, an organization committed to helping today's youth.

❀ **Relational Aggression**
   Behavior that is intended to harm someone by damaging or manipulating his or her relationships with others

❀ **Peer Aggression**
   Includes physical, verbal and relational aggression between youth near the same age or grade

❀ **Physical Aggression**
   Harm through damage or threat of damage to another's physical well being

❀ **Verbal Aggression**
   Obvious and hidden verbal acts of aggression, such as threats, putdowns and name calling

❀ **Overt Aggression**
   Obvious, blatant acts of aggression

❀ **Covert Aggression**
   Hidden acts of aggression (e.g. body language, exclusion, cyber bullying)

❀ **Reactive Relational Aggression**
   Defensive response to provocation with intent to retaliate

❀ **Proactive Relational Aggression**
   Proactive behaviors are a means for achieving a goal, for example, a girl may exclude someone to maintain her own social status (e.g. a girl is mad at another girl for being "more popular" so she spreads a sexual rumor about her to ruin her reputation)

Methods of Relational Aggression

❀ Exclusion

❀ Ignoring

❀ Spreading Rumors

❀ Verbal Insults

❀ Teasing

❀ Eye Rolling

❀ Taunting

❀ Manipulative Affection

❀ Three Way Calling

❀ Video Phoning

❀ Cyber Bullying

Cyber-Bullying

Internet use is tremendous and is increasing. Although many girls may use the internet for educational purposes and to link to resources, there are just as many who use the internet to bully others. The internet is "hot" for many reasons. It can be used anonymously, it can be accessed 24/7, and it reaches mass audiences. Girls use the internet as a part of their social lifeline.

What is Cyber-Bullying?

"Using the Internet or other mobile devices to send or post harmful or cruel text or images to bully others."

— Nancy Willard, Director, Center for Safe and Responsible Internet Use

Cyber-Bullying and Girls

This is the "wired" generation and girls are creative in their tactics to cyber-bully each other. They have their own cyber language and there are few limits to what girls will do to each other online. Cyber-Bullies or "net bullies," as they are sometimes referred to, use different methods when preying on their victims.

The following are the most common forms of cyber-bullying:
- Instant messaging
- Chat rooms or discussion group
- Web pages
- Web logs (blogs)
- E-mails
- Text or digital imaging messages sent on cell phones

Kowalski (2005) conducted a study involving 6th, 7th, and 8th graders. He reported that Instant Messaging was the most common form of cyber-bullying by children/adolescents in grades 6-8. Other common forms included chat rooms, e-mails, and messages posted on websites. Kowalski also reported that girls are about twice as likely to be the victims and the perpetrators of cyber-bullying.

Kowalski's report provides the following statistics concerning victimization via the internet:

- 58% were victims of IM
- 28% were bullied in a chat room
- 20% were bullied on a web site
- 19% were bullied through e-mail
- 14% were bullied through text messaging

Cyber-Bullying (cont.)

Examples of Cyber-Bullying
- ❀ Sending cruel or threatening messages
- ❀ Creating websites that have stories, cartoons, pictures and jokes ridiculing others
- ❀ Posting pictures of classmates online and asking C/A to rate them
- ❀ Breaking into an e-mail account and sending vicious or embarrassing material to others
- ❀ Engaging someone in IM and tricking that person into revealing sensitive info, and forwarding it to others
- ❀ Taking a picture of a person in the locker room using a digital phone camera and sending that picture to others

---

How Technologically Savvy are you?

Let's look at how girls communicate and with what device.

"Text Messaging" (or SMS)
Text messaging or "short text-messages" are words and symbols used to communicate from mobile phones.

"E-Mail"
Short for electronic mail, it is the transmission of messages over electronic communication networks.

"IMing"- Short for Instant Messaging.
This is a private chat session with another individual.

"Chat Rooms or Bash Boards"
Similar to "IMing," it is "real-time" communication with someone using a computer. Various symbols, codes and acronyms are used to communicate. Bash Boards are online bulletin boards used anonymously to write anything you want about someone, true or not.

"MMS"- Short for Multimedia Messaging Service.
These messages combine the use of text, sounds, images and video to send messages to mobile phones with the appropriate capabilities.

"Voting or Polling Booths"
These allow for "free voting" such as "Who is the ugliest or the fattest, etc…at school."

"Web Sites"
In this day and age of technology anyone can have their own web site. Many girls have their own web page where almost anything can be posted.

Cyber "Language"

Cyber space is full of language that truly seems "out of this world." The following are abbreviations and symbols girls may use to communicate.

Cyber Space Acronyms:

4GM -Forgive me
AAMOF -As a matter of fact
AFK -Away from keyboard
ASL -Age, sex, location?
ASLP -Age, sex, location, picture?
ATYS -Anything you say
BFD -Big freakin' deal
BF -Boyfriend
BFN -Bye for now
BC -Be cool
B/C -Because
EG -Evil grin
EOD -End of discussion
EOL -End of lecture
EOR -End of rant
F -Female
F2F -Face to face
FCOL -For crying out loud
FITB -Fill in the blanks
FOCL -Falling off the chair laughing
FOFL -Falling on the floor laughing
FWIW -For what it's worth
FYA -For your amusement
FYI -For your information
G -Grin
G2G -Gotta go
GA -Good afternoon / Go ahead
GAL -Get a life
GF -Girlfriend
GFN -Gone for now
GI -Good idea
GIWISI -Gee, I wish I said it
GJ -Good job
GL -Good luck
GM -Good morning / Good move/match
GMTA -Great minds think alike
GN -Good night
GR8 -Great
H -Hug
HB -Hug back
H&K -Hugs and Kisses
HAGD -Have a good day
HCIT -How cool is that
HF -Have fun
HH -Ha-ha
HHSF -Ha-ha, so funny
HHVF -Ha-ha, very funny
HOAS -Hold on a second
IAC -In any case
IAG -It's all good
IAGW -In a good way
IC -I see / In character

IDGI -I don't get it
IDNDT -I did not do that
IIRC -If I remember correctly
IK -I know
IKWUM -I know what you mean
IMAO -In my arrogant opinion
IME -In my experience.
IMHO -In my humble opinion
IMNSHO -In my not so humble
    opinion
INRS -It's not rocket science
IOW -In other words
IRL -In real life
IRSTBO -It really sucks the big one
IS -I'm sorry
ISWYM -I see what you mean
JMHO -Just my humble opinion
JTLYK -Just to let you know
J/K -Just kidding
J/P -Just playing
K -OK
KIR -Keepin' it real
KIT -Keep in touch
KWIM -Know what I mean?
L8R -Later
LMK -Let me know
LTR -Long term relationship
LYK -Let you know
LMAO -Laughing my a•• off
LMBO -Laughing my butt off
LOL -Laugh out loud
LTNS -Long time no see
M -Male
MMA -Meet me at ...
MMAMP -Meet me at my place
MYOB -Mind your own business
N -In
NBD -No big deal
N2M -Not too much
N/C -Not cool
NE1 -Anyone
NM -Nevermind, Not much
NMH -Not much here
NMJC -Nothing much, just chillin'
NNITO -Not necessarily in that order
NO1 -No one
NOTTOMH -Not off the top of
    my head
NOYB -None of your business
NP -No problem
NRN -No reply necessary
NW -No way

OIC -Oh, I see
OMG -Oh my gosh
OOC -Out of character
OT -Off topic / Other topic
PLZ -Please
PPL -People
POS -Parent over shoulder
QT -Cutie
RESQ -Rescue
RFC -Request for comment
RHIP -Rank hath its privileges
ROF -Rolling on the floor
ROTFL -Rolling on the floor laughing
RTFM -Read the flippin' manual
S2R -Send to receive
SCNR -Sorry, could not resist
SLY -Still love you
SWALK -Sweet, with all love, kisses
SWAK -Sealed with a kiss
SYSOP -System Operator
TCO -Taken care of
TOH -The other half
THX -Thanks
TNX -Thanks
TIA -Thanks in advance
TMA -Take my advice
TMI -Too much information
TTFN -Ta ta for now
TTYL -Talk to you later
TY -Thank you
TYVM -Thank you very much
U2 -You too
UR -You are ...
VBG -Very big grin
W2F -Way too funny
W8 -Wait
W8AM -Wait a minute
WB -Welcome back OR Write back
WE -Whatever
WNDITWB -We never did it this
    way before
WRT -With Regard To
WTF -What the freak?
WTG -Way to go!
XOXOXO -Hugs and kisses
Y -Why?
YRG -You are good!
YW -You're welcome
>U! -Screw you!
? -Huh?
?4U -Question for you

Emoticons

Emoticons are facial expressions created by using different keystrokes.

!-(Black eye	%+{ Got beat up	%-| Worked all night
!-) Proud of black eye	%-(Confused	%-} Humorous or ironic
#-) Wiped out, partied all night	%-) Dazed or silly	%\\ Hangover
#:-o Shocked	%-6 Brain-dead	>>:-<< Furious
%*} Inebriated	%-\\ Hung over	>- Female
	%-{ Ironic	

PREVENTION AND INTERVENTION IN COMBATING CYBER-BULLYING

Advice for Educators

❀ Educate faculty, staff and students about cyber-bullying, its effects and dangers.

❀ Address cyber-bullying in the school anti-bullying policies and procedures.

❀ Observe students' use of computers at school.

❀ Utilize filtering and tracking software on all computers; however, this will not always prevent cyber-bullying from taking place.

❀ If you become aware of cyber-bullying taking place on your school campus, look into the situation and report your findings. Know your district policy on reporting.

❀ If you become aware of cyber-bullying occurring away from school, consider your options based on the information. Actions you could take to address the bullying include:
  • Notify parents of victims and of cyber-bullies and share the information discovered about cyber-bullying.
  • If the cyber-bullying involved threats or other inappropriate criminal behavior, notify the police.
  • Educate all students about the harm caused by cyber-bullying.

❀ Follow up with victims of cyber-bullying and refer to a school counselor or outside counselor if needed.

❀ Immediately contact law enforcement if the cyber-bullying involves any of the following:
  • Threats of violence
  • Extortion
  • Obscene or harassing phone calls or text messages
  • Harassment, stalking, or hate crimes
  • Child pornography

Web Sites and Resources of Interest

The internet has increasingly become a primary method of communication for children and adolescents; the following web sites may help you navigate and find insight into their world. This is a very small sampling.

* www.hateboard.com

* www.myspace.com

* www.xanga.com

* www.teenangels.com

* www.schoolscandal.com

* www.livejournal.com

Helpful Websites:

* www.transl8it.com – a website to help to translate text messages or SMS

* www.webopedia.com – an online dictionary to help you navigate online terminology and acronyms

* www.whatis.com – helps you define all those "techno" terms

Statistics

In order to progress through the developmental stages successfully, children and adolescents need to feel a sense of belonging, competency, control and power. Relational aggression interrupts this process.

Adolescents are an important group to study given that involvement in relational aggression has been shown to escalate during this time period (Owens et al., 2000; Werner and Hill, 2004). Peer status, approval, identity, intimacy, as well as a sense of belonging, are all salient issues for adolescents. These normative developmental tasks may lead to confusion, increased peer competition, and selfish ambition, making the ground particularly fertile for relational aggression (Wiseman, 2002).

While this age group is an important one to study, research from Brigham Young University (2005) reports that girl bullying starts as early as preschool. In 2005 researchers at the University of Montreal, University of Quebec at Montreal and Laval University in Canada studied 234 sets of six year old twins. Their research found that 80% of a child's relationally aggressive behavior is due to environmental factors such as parenting and peer influence. Dr. Mara Brendgen reports that " ...60% of genetics determine whether you are aggressive or not, but this aggressiveness is initially expressed as physical aggressiveness. The environment determines whether you make the shift from physical to social aggressiveness" (Brendgen, et al. 2005).

Children are the targets of bullying about once every three to six minutes from the start of kindergarten to the end of first grade, according to a November 2003 report released by the Center for the Advancement of Health and supported by the National Institute of Mental Health.

In 2005 UCLA researchers conducted a study in middle school settings and defined bullying as behaviors that include "... name calling, making fun of others, spreading nasty rumors and physical aggression." They discovered that 50% of the children engaged in the study reported being bullied during a five day period. They also found that children are hesitant to report aggressive behavior and may instead seek out the school nurse for complaints concerning various symptoms (Juvonen et al., 2005).

Relational aggression is seen in our children at an early age and will continue throughout their childhood unless we provide education, increase awareness and teach alternative solutions for their behavior. We have a responsibility to address these issues in a systemic way in order to give our children and adolescents the best possible chance to overcome this hurtful behavior.

Short and Long Term Effects of Relational Aggression:

Relational aggression is behavior that can have a negative impact that can last a lifetime. The following are possible effects of RA in elementary, middle and high school youth:

- Depression
- Loneliness/Isolation
- Suicidal Ideation
- Interrupted Identity Formation
- Poor Self-Esteem
- Feelings of Powerlessness
- Inappropriate Feelings of Power
- Inability to Trust
- Poor Relational Skills
- Anger
- Hostility/Physical Aggression
- Frustration
- Helplessness
- Hopelessness
- Feelings of rejection
- Stress
- Anxiety
- Separation Anxiety
- Teen Pregnancy
- Substance Abuse
- Self-Injury
- Eating Disorders
- Homicidal Ideation
- Death

Relational Aggression not only affects students; it also has a negative impact on the school. The environment in which you teach, guide, and nurture these students unfortunately becomes infected with the poison of RA. The following are a few of the effects of RA on your school:

- Poor academic performance
- Delinquent Behavior
- Absenteeism/Truancy
- Increased disciplinary actions
- Frustrations for faculty and staff
- An environment of fear and disrespect

Misguided Interventions in Approaching Relational Aggression

* **Conflict Mediation:**
According to Richard Cohen in "The School Mediator" Dan Olweus and his colleagues state, "Conflict between bullies and their victims should not be mediated, especially not by students" With RA, there is an imbalance of power. However well intentioned, by encouraging conflict mediation you are sending the message that the victim is equally responsible for the behavior.

* **Peer Mediation:**
Bullying is not a conflict; it is abuse. There is not right and wrong on both sides. Having peers mediate a situation of RA again implies a responsibility on the part of the victim for the abuse.

* **Groups made up of only RA girls:**
The RA girls will begin to "one up" each other and will reinforce the RA behavior.

* **Zero Tolerance Policy:**
Policies of this type are created for disciplinary problems that warrant suspension or expulsion from school. Because of the extreme punishment, students and adults alike are hesitant to report RA behavior. Suspension and expulsion may be necessary in some cases to protect other students, however a zero tolerance policy should not be utilized as an RA policy.

101½ Creative Strategies and Activities for Working with Relational Aggression

In this section, we have provided four different relational aggression assessment tools for you to use. Assessments are an important part of the process to determine the level of relational aggression in your students and at your school. In addition, the Sisterhood Survey on page 26 will help bring insight and awareness to the girls you work with.

Strategies 1-4
Assessing Who's Who: Tools You Can Use

Relational Aggression Survey

Use this reproducible survey to identify relational aggression in your school. The survey will help your school discover the dynamics of RA, specifically where it takes place, who is involved and the tactics used. Collecting data is the first step in finding solutions or seeing if the policies and procedures you have in place are effective.

Prior to the survey being taken be sure that the C/A's have a clear definition of RA and several examples of RA. The questions are designed for children and adolescents and the results are easy to analyze. The survey may need to be verbally given to grades that are beginning to read and they can record their responses privately.

It is very important that the surveys be anonymous. Inform C/A's that they will not be identified by name, only by class. Soon after the surveys are completed have someone begin to go through them to see if there are any specific requests for help in a particular class. If there are any special requests, have the professional counselor address RA with the class to talk with them about the importance of talking to an adult. Help them to identify safe adults that they can talk with.

Once you have compiled your results share them with faculty and staff. Also, share them with C/A's. As you begin to build a team of people to address RA, include several of the C/A's as their insight will be valuable in the overall success of your program.

Relational Aggression Survey

Directions: Please **DO NOT** put your name anywhere on the following survey.

You are allowed to write anything in this survey that you feel would be helpful for us to better address relational aggression at our school.

We want to know what you think about relational aggression. The answers to the questions below will help us to stop relational aggression.

To help you have a clearer understand about Relational Aggression we have included a definition.

Relational Aggression (RA) is bullying:
It takes on many different forms. It can be someone talking behind your back, picking on you or teasing you, not allowing you in their group, text messaging or instant messaging about you, verbally insulting or threatening you. These are just a few of the ways that relational aggression may be seen or felt. Relational Aggression is one sided in its power, for example one girl uses her power negatively to make another girl feel hurt or bad about herself. Relational aggression harms other people.

Share with us what you think about relational aggression at our school.

What is your.....

Age_____

Grade_____

Ethnicity_____

Who is your....

Teacher_____

Please put a check mark beside the answers that best apply. If there is not an answer you think works best you may use the blank space to write in your response.

1. Have you ever participated in relational aggression (girl bullying)?

    ❏ No, I have never participated in RA

    ❏ Yes, I have participated in RA

    ❏ If yes, then have you participated in RA ❏ Daily ❏ Weekly ❏ Monthly

2. What role did you play in RA?

    ❏ I have never been involved in RA

    ❏ Instigator

    ❏ Participant

    ❏ Observer/Bystander

3. Have you ever been the target of RA?

    ❏ No, I have never been the target of RA

    ❏ Yes, I have been the target of RA

    ❏ If yes, were you most recently targeted

      ❏ Within the last week ❏ Within the last month ❏ Within the last year

4. What kind of RA (girl bullying) was it? *(check all that apply)*

    ❏ I have never experienced RA

    ❏ Name calling

    ❏ Excluded or left out by others

    ❏ Teased

    ❏ Gossip

    ❏ Threatened

    ❏ Text messages, Emails or Instant Messaging

    ❏ Physical aggression (hitting, slapping, pushing, etc…)

    ❏ Picked on for my looks

    ❏ Harassed because of my race or religion

    ❏ Comments or verbal taunts related to homosexuality

    ❏ Rumors spread about me

    ❏ Three way calls

    ❏ Other (explain) _____

5. Where did the relational aggression (girl bullying) happen? *(check all that apply)*

  ❏ I have never experienced RA

  ❏ On the way to school (on the bus, walking in)

  ❏ In the hallway

  ❏ In the lunch area

  ❏ On the playground

  ❏ In a classroom

  ❏ In the restroom

  ❏ In the locker room

  ❏ On the internet

  ❏ On the phone (cell phone, three way call)

  ❏ Other _____

6. Did you tell anyone about the relational aggression (girl bullying)? *(check all that apply)*

  ❏ I have never experienced RA

  ❏ Yes, my friend

  ❏ Yes, a teacher

  ❏ Yes, an adult I trust

  ❏ Yes, my parent

  ❏ Yes, my sister/brother

  ❏ No, I did not tell anyone

  ❏ No, there is no one to tell

  ❏ No, telling is not cool

  ❏ No, even if I told no one would do anything

7. If you told someone, what happened when you told him/her? *(check all that apply)*

❑ I did not tell anyone

❑ I felt better

❑ The person helped me know what to do

❑ The person did something to stop the RA
What did that person do to stop the RA? _____

_____

_____

❑ The person did something but the RA did not stop
What did that person do to try to stop the RA? _____

_____

_____

❑ The person did something but it made the RA worse
What did that person do that made it worse? _____

_____

_____

❑ Nothing was done but the RA has stopped
What do you think made the RA stop? _____

_____

_____

❑ Nothing was done and the RA continues to happen

❑ I feel they do not know what to do

Is there anything you feel would help RA stop? _____

_____

_____

8. If you have ever been involved in or witnessed a relational aggression (girl bullying) incident, what did you do?

❏ I have never been involved in a relational aggression incident

❏ My friends and I talk about other girls

❏ Teased another girl

❏ Called her names

❏ Rolled my eyes at her

❏ Didn't invite her to my party

❏ Wouldn't let her sit or hang out with the group

❏ Posted something negative on the internet

❏ IM'd anonymously

❏ Gossiped about another girl

❏ Spread rumors about someone

❏ Laughed at someone else's joke about a girl

❏ Watched another girl taunt someone

❏ Told someone they were not welcome

❏ Written a note about someone that wasn't nice

❏ Refused to talk to another girl

❏ Repeated something I heard about another girl

❏ E-mailed someone a negative message

❏ Posted negative messages in a chat room about someone

❏ Made fun of the way someone was dressed

❏ Intentionally embarrassed someone

❏ Insulted someone

❏ I did nothing

❏ Other

9. If you have ever experienced RA (girl bullying), been a victim or target, what did you do in this situation?

❏ I laughed it off

❏ I panicked and ran

❏ I got embarrassed and turned red in the face

❏ I acted like it didn't bother me

❏ I stood up for myself
Specifically what did you do to stand up for yourself? _____

❏ I tried to stay away from those girls

❏ I did not come to school

❏ I just dealt with it by myself

❏ I made new friends

❏ I did nothing

10. Have you ever missed school because someone was relationally aggressive towards you?

❏ Yes

❏ No

11. Do you know about your school's policy regarding Relational Aggression?

❏ Yes

❏ Sort of

❏ No

❏ I don't know if my school has a policy

❏ My school does not have a policy

12. Do you think that your school is doing everything it can to address Relational Aggression?
(check all that apply)

❏ Yes

❏ In some ways

❏ No

Do you have any suggestions for your school that you think could help? _____

_____

_____

13. Is there anything else you would like to share or any ideas you have to address Relational Aggression?

_____

_____

_____

_____

Thank you for answering these questions.

Sisterhood Survey: Who are you?

Answer the following to find out...

(circle your response)

1. **You notice a girl sitting alone in the cafeteria, you...**
   a. think "oh what a loser."
   b. feel sorry for her, but your friends will be mad if you ask her to sit with you.
   c. ask her to sit with you and your friends.

2. **You like the outfit a girl has on, you...**
   a. think to yourself " oh she thinks she looks so good" and roll your eyes.
   b. make a negative comment to your friends just so you will look cool.
   c. compliment her on her outfit.

3. **You see a girl crying in the bathroom, you...**
   a. laugh with your friends because her eyes are red and her face is all puffy.
   b. feel sorry for her, but you're afraid to reach out to her because of what your friends might say.
   c. ask her what is wrong and if there is anything you can do for her.

4. **You know there is one girl who is always picked on and teased, you...**
   a. think, "She's so weird, no wonder people pick on her."
   b. laugh with your friends, thankful that it is not you.
   c. stand up for her when you see this happening.

5. **A new girl arrives at your school and she is beautiful and wealthy, you...**
   a. think, "I cannot afford for her to take my place at the top."
   b. think, "It won't take long for her to become popular."
   c. think, "wow, she's really pretty, I know she's new, I wonder if she would like to hang out with me and my friends."

6. **You are on the internet IM'ing with your friends and they suggest you send a message you know is not true about a girl, you...**

   a. think, "great idea, she deserves it."

   b. add your own twist to the message even though you don't agree with what they are saying.

   c. tell them you will not send the message because you know it is not true.

7. **Your school counselor has asked you to be a part of a student team that will be trained to help girls that have been hurt by relational aggression, you...**

   a. tell him/her you are too busy to be part of the group but you hope they succeed at helping all those poor girls.

   b. wish you could be part of the group but your friends would totally ostracize you.

   c. tell him/her that you would love to be a part of the group.

8. **Your school starts an Anti-Relational Aggression program, you...**

   a. think that is so stupid and lame.

   b. think it is a good idea but would never admit it to your friends.

   c. think it's about time, there are too many mean girls at our school.

Give each letter a number value using the following scale:
A = 1   B = 2   C = 3

Here's your Sisterhood Score.

22-24: You Go Girl!!
You are the Queen of Nice! You feel good about yourself and strong in your character. You know what you stand for, and we need more of you in the Sisterhood! Keep it up, Girlfriend!

15-21: Hang on Girlfriend!
Your view of Sisterhood has surely got you in turmoil! You seem to have the right heart but the wrong actions. Hanging with those girls you call friends is only adding to the meanness we don't need in the Sisterhood. These girls are not really true friends. They only like you because you play their game. Try a hand at your own game and go with your gut!

8-14: Sister, you are the Queen of Mean!
Whoa, we need to chat!! You are destroying the Sisterhood and depriving yourself of having truly meaningful relationships. Girls were not created to destroy each other but to delight in our bond as sisters. Let's figure out where all this meanness is coming from and bring you into the Sisterhood where empathy and loyalty prevail! Look forward to seeing you soon!

The Color Continuum

❋ Overview:
School personnel as well as children/adolescents (C/A) can conduct a creative assessment of relational aggression using the Color Continuum.

❋ Materials Needed:
• Color Continuum worksheet
• Pen or pencil

❋ Procedure:
The Color Continuum identifies levels of aggression using colors. As a professional, you can use the Color Continuum to compare the C/A's behavior to that of the example behaviors listed in the left hand column on the Color Continuum worksheet. Fill in the C/A's behavior in the right hand column. Then determine where they fall on this continuum.

You can also use the continuum to discern a girl's perception of relationally aggressive behaviors and how they affect her. Have her define RA behaviors in terms of her perception of the impact in her life and where they would fall on the continuum. Then have her fill in her response next to the corresponding color.

❋ Discussion:
Discuss with the C/A the differences in her perceptions of relational aggression to those in the example boxes.
• In what way are they different from the Color Continuum?
• Explore with the C/A her personal experiences with relational aggression.
• Has she ever been a victim of RA?

❋ Follow Up:
Educate C/A about the impact of RA and how it affects others no matter where it may fall on the continuum.

The Color Continuum Worksheet

Identifying Levels of Aggression

1	2	3	4	5	6	7	8	9
Yellow		Green		Blue		Orange		Red

YELLOW

Eye rolling,
covert name calling,
putdowns

GREEN

Rumors,
gossip,
covert insults

BLUE

Backstabbing,
ostracizing,
ignoring

ORANGE

Threats,
taunting,
cyber bullying

RED

Hitting, slapping,
kicking, weapons,
video aggression

Assessing Emotional Needs

Based on the book *The Five Love Languages*, Dr. Gary Chapman reports that we all have a primary love language. The five love languages are Quality Time, Words of Affirmation, Physical Touch, Acts of Service and Gifts. Discovering ones love language fulfills the basic need for experiencing love. (Chapman, G., 1995)

Most people are completely unaware they have emotional needs, especially our youth, hence we have a society of individuals just existing and feeling unloved.

As we know there is no universal mold for children and adolescents therefore we must accept each one as unique and having much to offer. It is in the discovery of this uniqueness that their specific emotional needs may begin to emerge.

Children need words of encouragement daily to affirm their worth and show them acceptance of **who** they are and not **what** they do. Some children may respond well to hugs or positive pats on the back while others soak up your undivided attention and enjoy spending time with you. Many others feel loved when something special is done for them or a token gift is given to them. The underlying message for all is unconditional love.

To begin to discover the needs of the girls you work with, consider asking a few thought provoking and open ended questions. Use the following questions to guide you in identifying their individual needs.

Emotional Needs Assessment Guide

Ask the child or adolescent you are working with the following questions.

❋ **Who is your best friend?** _____

❋ **How does your friend show you she is your best friend?**
(For example, does she write you nice notes or compliment your achievements, does she give you gifts or tokens of appreciation, does she spend time with you and listen if you have a problem, etc.)

_____

_____

❋ **What do you do for your best friend to let him/her know he/she is special or important to you?**

_____

_____

❋ **If you were going to do something kind for someone, what would you do?** _____

_____

_____

The C/A's needs will begin to emerge through the answers to these questions. For example, if the C/A answers that her best friend says nice things about her and always gives her encouraging notes, then you will see that child responds well to words of encouragement or affirmation. You may also want to observe C/A as you spend time with her. Does she respond well to your words of praise, tokens of appreciation, hugs or encouraging touch, time spent with you or your help with a situation? Helping her realize the emotional needs in her life and how to have them met will be paramount in her survival of daily life.

Based on the book *The Five Love Languages*, Dr. Gary Chapman (1995), reports that we all have a primary love language. Discovering that love language fulfills the basic need for experiencing love. The five love languages are Quality Time, Words of Affirmation, Physical Touch, Acts of Service and Gifts. Seek out in your C/A what her love language may be.

101½ Creative Strategies and Activities for Working with Relational Aggression

Individual counseling by a school counselor or a licensed professional, help the child/adolescent explore and resolve personal problems caused by relational aggression. Individual counseling allows the child/adolescent to explore her feelings, behaviors and motives towards her relationships with others. The counselor can also help her to explore the underlying issues that caused the relational aggression and ways to resolve it.

When utilizing the individual strategies in this section, you can help bring about insight and change into the behaviors associated with relational aggression. These strategies are designed for all girls: for the aggressor, the target and the bystander.

Strategies 5-35
Individual Interventions

S T R A T E G Y   5

Picture Mixture

❋ Overview:

What you see on the outside does not always reflect what is actually on the inside.

❋ Materials Needed:

- 8.5 x 11 piece of paper
- Colored markers, pencils or crayons

❋ Procedure:

Have the C/A and another person (either another C/A or an adult) each draw a picture that is large enough to fill the page. They may choose to draw whatever they like, but cannot reveal the pictures they are drawing. Then have them fold the piece of paper nine times accordion/fan style.

Have the C/A trade her picture with the other person and have them lay the pictures face up without stretching the accordion. Have them guess what they think the drawing represents. They should not be able to discern what is within the folds.

❋ Follow Up:

Discuss with the C/A the concept that we don't always know the whole "picture" of someone's life or circumstances. Just like the drawing, we only see parts of another person's life. Discuss with the C/A the importance of empathy when considering other peers' feelings. Brainstorm examples of how to look at the "whole picture" before making assumptions about others.

What's in your closet?

● **Overview:**

Often children/adolescents hide emotions they do not want anyone to see. Help C/A learn how to express these emotions appropriately so she is not "hiding" in the closet.

● **Materials Needed:**

• Closet worksheet on the following page
• Pens, colored pencils, crayons or markers

● **Procedure:**

Have the C/A write emotion words in her closet related to how she feels about school, friends, peers, cliques, relationships etc. The closet should include both pleasant and unpleasant emotions.

● **Follow Up:**

Explore with the C/A any emotions that she may be hiding inside that she doesn't want anyone to see. Discuss with the C/A any barriers she has in expressing her emotions. Help C/A learn how to express these emotions appropriately so she is not "hiding" in the closet. Help the C/A identify people with whom she feels safe in sharing her emotions.

What's in your closet?

Write emotion words here:

Inside Out

Discovering and Learning How to be Your Authentic Self

❀ Overview:

Many times girls experience being judged for the way they look on the outside, by perceptions people have or by an image they themselves try to project. This strategy will help reveal who the C/A really is on the inside and help her work toward becoming her authentic self.

❀ Materials Needed:

- 8 1/2x11 or 11x14 blank piece of paper
- Pens, colored pencils, crayons or markers

❀ Procedure:

Have the (C/A) place the blank paper flat in front of her so it is in a horizontal position. Then have the C/A make two folds so each fold meets in the center of the page. You should have two panels that you can open. Instruct the C/A to draw a picture or write words on the outside of the paper describing the perceptions that other people have of her. Then on the inside of the paper, have the C/A draw a picture or write words describing who she believes she really is. Discuss the differences in the two pictures.

❀ Follow Up:

- Have the C/A discuss the reasons for the differences in the two pictures.
- Have the C/A discuss different ways to be who she really is.
- Is she happy with what she sees? If so...why? If not...why not?

Outside Drawing

Inside Drawing

S T R A T E G Y 8

Thunder and Lightning

❀ When someone says something ugly or gives you a mean look, it's like a strike of lightning to your soul. Immediately begin to count… one hippopotamus in a tutu….two hippopotamus in a tutu….three hippopotamus in a tutu, etc. In doing this it will help keep the thunderous reaction from coming on or to help "count" yourself out of the situation. Share with someone situations when this strategy might help.

Mighty Finger: The Power of One

❂ Overview:

There are times C/A's struggle to find their identity. Help them identify their unique characteristics.

❂ Materials Needed:

- Plain piece of paper
- Ink Pad
- Pens, pencils, crayons or markers

❂ Procedure:

Using the ink pad have the C/A put their thumb print on the paper. Using their thumb print they can decorate the print by drawing animal faces, flowers, or something she feels represents who she is. Share with the C/A that no two people have the exact same finger print. Every finger print is completely different. Have C/A list two special traits that make her different. Help her see these traits make her unique. Encourage C/A to be proud of her unique characteristics by giving herself a "thumbs up" once in a while.

❂ Follow Up:

Allow each girl to share their special traits. Discuss different ways to validate and encourage each other.

Magic Spiral

❋ Overview:

We all look different from many different angles and may look different every time.
Seeing ourselves from all angles helps us better understand who we are.

❋ Materials Needed:

• Magic Spiral worksheet
• Pens, pencils, crayons or markers

❋ Procedure:

Using the worksheet have the C/A color the circle, list words that describe herself on each spiral,
then cut it out. Punch a hole in the top at the center and pull a string through the top. It is now a
hanging mobile. Watch as the mobile begins to twist and turn….from every angle it looks a little
different. Have C/A share how she can appear different at different times to different people.

❋ Follow Up:

What are the positives of looking at ourselves from all angles? What can we learn about what we see?
Discuss with the C/A that she looks different from many different angles and may even
look different every time. Looking at ourselves from all angles gives us an opportunity to grow and
develop and discover new things about ourselves.

Magic Spiral

Song and Dance

❀ Overview:

It can be fun to "dance to the beat of your own drum." But what does that really mean? Finding what makes girls different will help them keep up the dance of life.

❀ Materials Needed:

• CD Player and various snippets of different types of music
  (country, rock, classical, rap, rock n'roll, pop, etc…)

❀ Procedure:

Play the snippets of music.

❀ Follow Up:

Ask the C/A which type of music she liked best. Maybe share your favorite type of music. We all like music, however we do not all like the same type of music. Our relationships are much the same way. We know our friends like music but as friends we may not always like the same kind. Explore with the C/A what it means to "dance to the beat of your own drum." Have her write 3 ways she feels she is unique and dance to the beat of her own drum.

Sugar Sparks

"Sugar and spice and everything nice"

❋ Growing up we are taught to "be nice," and many girls are never taught how to deal appropriately with emotions such as anger or disappointment. So, in an attempt to convey how they feel, many girls become socially aggressive or express other negative behaviors.

❋ Have a discussion with the girls and ask them the following questions. Ask each to respond by either writing a response or verbally sharing how they feel about each one.

1. What does the statement "sugar and spice and everything nice" mean to you?

2. In what way do you act "nice" when you are really feeling another emotion?

3. What are some respectful ways to express unpleasant emotions such as disappointment, frustration, or sadness?

4. Do you think that being told to grow up "nice" could contribute to girls being relationally aggressive? (You may need to define RA)

5. Do you think girls can change the way they treat each other? How? List three ways.

❋ Challenge each girl to put into action the suggestions they shared.

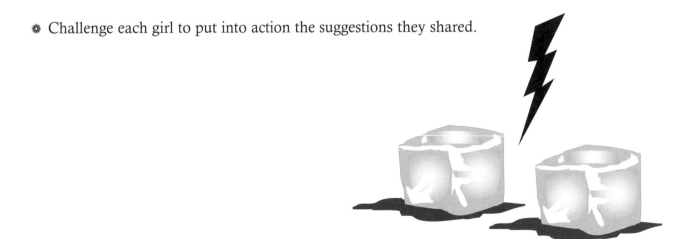

Parachute

❀ Overview:

When jumping from an airplane it's good to know you have a parachute! In theory, parachutes work by opposing forces of friction and gravity. Using this theory teach, C/A how she can oppose the aggression that may be inflicted upon them from others.

❀ Materials Needed:

- A plastic sandwich bag
- Scissors
- String
- Small item of weight(ex. A key, a small toy figure)

❀ Procedures:

Take the sandwich bag and cut into a square. Then punch holes in the four corners and attach string. On the opposite end tie the string to a small item of weight. Throw this in the air and watch the parachute descend. Have the girls hold up their parachutes. Give examples of how other girls can be relationally aggressive. Once the C/A thinks of a positive way to handle the situation, have her drop her parachute. Then share the strategy with everyone.

❀ Discussion:

- What are some ways you can oppose RA?
- Have the C/A list these solutions and discuss how to put them into action.
- Who is someone you can count on to help you?

❀ Variation:

If you have a group of C/A, have them role play how they would oppose relational aggression.

S T R A T E G Y 1 4

Mirror Mirror

❀ Overview:

The reflection of what others see may not be the actual image of who we are.

❀ Materials Needed:

• Mirror Mirror Worksheet
• Pens, pencils

❀ Procedure:

Using the Mirror Mirror worksheet help the C/A gain insight into what she thinks she shows others versus what may be her true reflection.

On the left mirror have C/A list characteristics about herself and who she thinks she is.
Then on the right mirror, have the C/A list what she thinks others see in her.

❀ Follow Up:

Discuss with the C/A what she discovered in her "reflection." Do others see what is really there? Why or why not? Is she allowing her true self to be reflected? Why is trust important in revealing our true self? What are possible barriers in showing our "true" selves?

Mirror Mirror

What I Show Others....

What Others See....

S T R A T E G Y   1 5

Shining Star

❀ Do you cast a shadow… or shine? When you speak kindly to others, smile at others or include them in your group they see you shine. There may be times when it's hard to shine because of the hurtful things you may have done. When you gossip or use relationally aggressive behavior you do not shine; however, when you encourage or support others, speak kind words or include someone in your group, you shine in a way that reflects who you really are.

❀ How can you shine in a way that reflects who you really are?

❀ List three ways you shine:

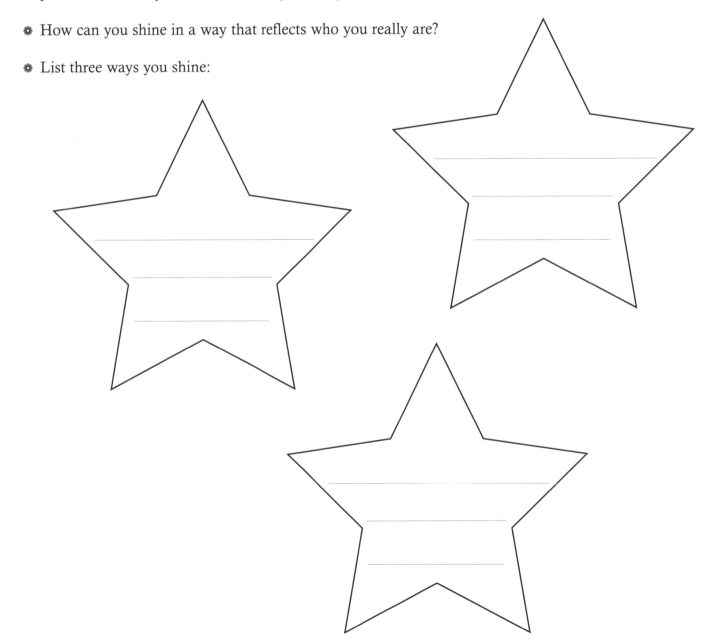

All in a Word

✹ Use the following words to see how many words are contained within the main word, for example using the word Character, you could find the words act, teach, care. Use these words as a springboard for a positive discussion. Discuss with the child or adolescent how choosing her words carefully and knowing the message they really send can have a positive or negative impact on the listener.

Thoughtfulness	Compassion	Admiration	Empathy	Kindness

Butterfly Surprise

❋ Overview:

Help C/A discover the characteristics that attract others to her.

❋ Materials Needed:

- Tin pan
- Dirt
- Water
- One cup of sugar
- Flower petals

❋ Procedure:

Mix the dirt and water in the tin pan to a muddy thickness. Stir in a large number of flower petals and the sugar. Put the "Butterfly Surprise" in the sun until it dries. Butterflies will be attracted to the mixture.

❋ Discussion Questions:

- What kind of people do you attract and how do you attract them?
- Do you attract others with your kindness or compassionate heart?
- Discuss ways you show kindness or compassion toward others.

❋ Follow Up:

What do you think attracted the butterflies to your Butterfly Surprise? Discuss the ingredients that are "sweet" and relate this to the concept of kindness and caring and behaviors that "attract" other's to us.

Watch for the butterflies and have fun!

Calculator Messages

❀ RA can be very calculating and mean spirited. Would you know how to recognize RA words?

❀ The following are a few examples
of RA statements or situations.

❀ Discuss how words can "add up" to hurt other people. How can the girl respond positively if caught in these situations. Help her choose more positive responses that can be multiplied and therefore hold a higher value.

Secret Code....Secret Sisters

* Within your school, identify those who have been victimized by RA or who want to learn more about standing strong in the face of RA by becoming "Secret Sisters." This is an opportunity to provide peer encouragement in combating RA. This will help inspire girls to be more supportive of each other and show the true meaning of sisterhood.

* Once you have identified a group of girls who are committed to being supportive and encouraging, brainstorm methods of communication that will encourage them throughout the day. For example, a hand signal that is encouraging, or one that signifies "My feelings are hurt." A variation of this would be to create a "secret code" based on a number/letter system such as a,b,c corresponding to the numbers 1,2,3.

* It is important that professionals facilitate a sense of belonging between the girls in the group so they feel connected to each other; however, it is also important to discuss ways to avoid making others feel excluded. Anyone can join and participate in the "Secret Code" and be a "Secret Sister."

"Hand"ling It

❂ Children and adolescents feel alone at times and helplessness paralyzes their ability to believe they have anyone who will be there for them. Help them to identify people who are available to lend a helping hand. This will remind them who they can count on in a time of need.

❂ Have the child or adolescent trace her hand and write on each finger the name of a person she feels could offer a "helping hand." Encourage her to include friends as well as adults. Also include on this list someone safe from her neighborhood. A variation of this activity would be to outline the child's hand and have her write down on each finger specific strategies she can use when she feels hurt from RA. Have the child/adolescent review these strategies with you.

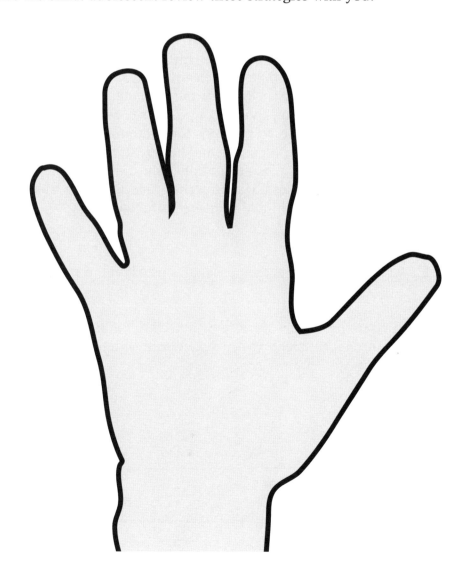

Bank It!!!

❋ **Overview:**

Learn to recognize positive interactions as well as negative interactions.

❋ **Materials Needed:**

• Bank It! worksheet

• Pen, pencil

❋ **Procedure:**

Interactions in relationships can be compared to a bank account. There are positive comments, actions, behaviors that when we experience them could be considered "deposits". Deposits are those things which nurture our spirit. It could be someone smiling at us, positive words, encouragement or a card out of the blue. On the other hand, there are negative and at times hurtful comments or behaviors that could be categorized as "withdrawals." Withdrawals affect us in a negative way. Examples could be, purposely being left out, insults, being a victim of gossip etc. Help the child/adolescent list interactions or events she would consider to be deposits or withdrawals in her life. This will help her really notice when deposits are occurring and be able to recognize withdrawals as well. On the worksheet that follows, have the C/A write out things she did within the last few days that could be considered "deposits" or "withdrawals." Have her share her list with a trusted friend or adult and discuss different ways to increase deposits and decrease withdrawals.

❋ **Follow Up:**

Explore with the C/A the reasons for the different things listed on the worksheet.

❋ **Variation:**

Have the C/A repeat the activity but this time she will need to think of different ways other people make deposits in her life and the different ways people create withdrawals.

Bank It!!!

Directions: Think about your interactions with others during the past week. Describe the deposits you were able to make and any withdrawals that you made.

WEEK OF	PERSON AFFECTED	DEPOSIT	WITHDRAWAL

The Force Field

❋ Overview:

Teach C/A to envision a "force field" to protect her from the harmful words or actions of others as well as her own need to "react."

❋ Materials Needed:

- "Force Field" worksheet
- Pen, pencil

❋ Procedure:

Relational aggression violates the boundaries of it's victims. It can be very hurtful. It may cause children/adolescents to react in ways that are hurtful to others as well. Discuss why boundaries are important and how we can use them to protect ourselves. Use examples of protective barriers such as a "force field," "haz mat" (hazardous material) suit, a castle with a moat, guard rails, basketball court, or lines on an athletic field such as softball or soccer field. On the Force Field worksheet that follows, have the C/A write hurtful words or behaviors that others have said or done to him.

❋ Follow Up:

Have the C/A talk about how these statements cannot penetrate the "force field." Discuss the importance of an imaginary force field for the hurtful words or actions of others to "bounce" off and not be harmful.

Force Field

Directions: On the lines below, write hurtful statements or actions that others have said or done to you.

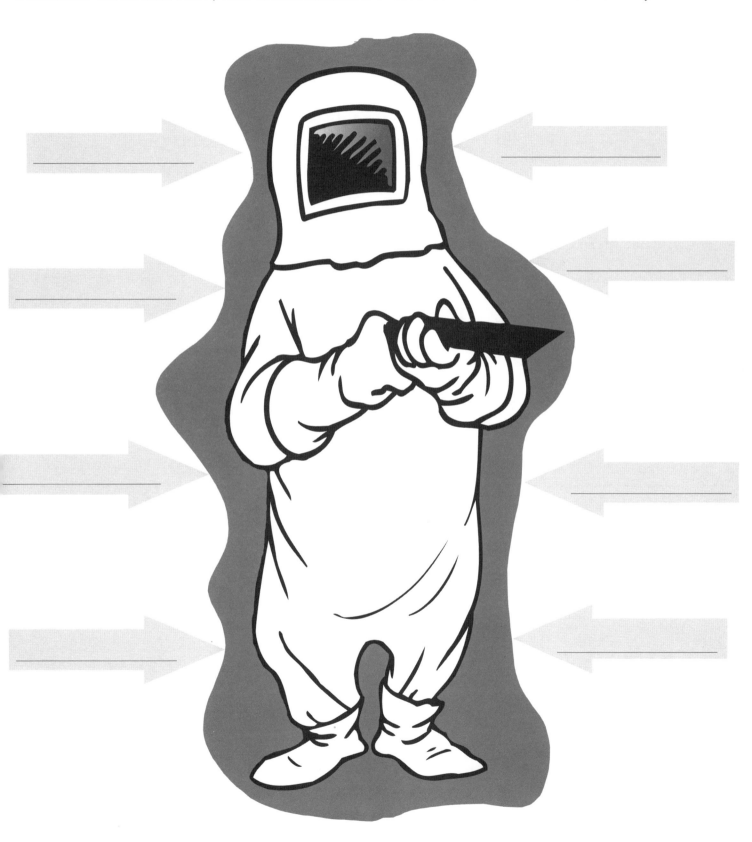

"Legacy"

A legacy is a lasting impression that you will leave behind for your family, friends or community.

❋ We have all heard the phrase "What will your legacy be?" How many people have given it serious thought and have actually written it out? This is a challenge to consider at this point in your life, "What will be your legacy?"

❋ **Consider these questions as you begin:**

• Will your legacy be positive? _____

• How do you want others to remember you? (you could interview a friend, teacher or family member to help you)

_____

_____

_____

_____

• List three ways you hope to be remembered.

_____

_____

_____

❋ For most of you, you are at a place in your life where you are just beginning to contribute to what will be your legacy. Challenge yourself to focus on the positive traits in your life and begin now practicing the legacy you want to leave behind.

"Genie in a Bottle"

Congratulations! You have been granted 3 wishes…

❋ This can be part fantasy part reality…but choose at least one wish that you CAN make come true!!

❋ Take time to sit and ponder what the wishes would be. Once you have decided what your wishes will be, think of someone else to give these wishes to. Then create a wish for someone else that you can actually make come true!

My Personal Mandala

❁ **A Mandala is a circular picture. It is made up of symbols or pictures.**

Have the C/A look through magazines and cut out symbols that represent who she is. Then paste these pictures on a circular piece of cardboard. Many party stores have these. Once this is finished, explore the meaning behind the symbols chosen. Ask the C/A "Who are you? Who do people see?" "Are they different and if so…why?" This can be a very insightful activity for students, designed to reveal who they think they really are.

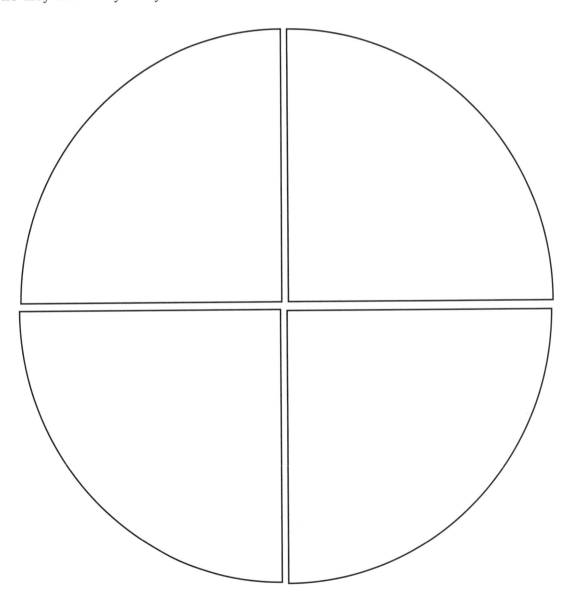

Girls..... Girls..... Girls.....

❋ It is important to understand the child/adolescent's perception of girls; girls they know, girls they see, girls they have heard of, girls in general.

❋ Have the child/adolescent finish the following sentences. Then discuss with her the themes that you may see as it relates to relational aggression. How do girls stereotype themselves? Are their thoughts positive or negative in relation to their gender?

❋ Have the C/A fill in the unfinished sentences below according to what she believes.

Girls are... _____

Girls can be... _____

Girls should be... _____

I am... _____

I can be... _____

I should be... _____

Magic Powers

❋ There are times when someone catches us off guard and we feel totally helpless in knowing how to respond. Each of us is equipped with the ability to respond but how do we make it magically appear when we need it? We must identify our inner strengths and how to make them magically appear when we need them!

List three personal strengths that you have:

1._____

2._____

3._____

(If you need a boost, here are some examples. A sense of humor, kind, creative, resilient, etc…)

❋ Now, put these three strengths on a sticky note and put them in a place you will see them often (ie. a notebook or agenda, in your purse or locker). Remind yourself daily of these strengths and watch them "magically" appear when you need them in a tough situation. One more note, you can add to this list to continually remind yourself of the many strengths you have.

The "Real" Cover Girl

NATURAL BEAUTY...ENHANCING WHO YOU ARE

* **Overview:**

  Help the C/A explore her inner beauty.

* **Materials Needed:**

  • The Real Cover Girl Worksheet
  • Pens, pencils

* **Procedure:**

  Have the C/A complete the Real Cover Girl Worksheet.
  Discuss with the C/A her responses and her reasons for those responses.

* **Follow Up:**

  Explore with the girl what she discovered about herself.
  • Did she learn anything new about herself?
  • What qualities make her interesting and unique?

  Have her continue to add to her interview and focus on the positive traits that make her a "real" cover girl, one who has natural beauty from the inside out and not "air brushed" to appear to be someone she is not.

The Real Cover Girl

You have just been chosen to be on the cover of a magazine! You have a few choices to make before your magazine hits the stands! The reporter needs information for the articles in the magazine where you will be featured. Help the reporter by completing the following information.

❀ **Describe the magazine you will be featured in:**

_____

_____

_____

❀ **Tell us about yourself:**

_____

_____

_____

❀ **Why do you think you have been chosen to be the Cover Girl?**

_____

_____

_____

❀ **What are a few interesting facts about yourself?**
   List at least three positive traits about yourself.

_____

_____

Why so Mean?

❈ Have the C/A write a story about a "mean girl". Ask her to include how the mean girl bullies other girls. Describe at least three reasons why she thinks the mean girl bullies others.

❈ Once the story is complete, discuss how she thinks the mean girl feels when she bullies others. What are some misconceptions that she may have about why mean girls bully?

❈ Encourage her to realize that mean girl behavior is about fear, insecurity and loss of control. Many times understanding the reasons why a behavior occurs helps us to be better prepared when dealing with that behavior.

❈ With these insights in mind, help the C/A create a personal plan for when she faces relational aggression. Have her list four ways she can use these insights.

Walkin' in Her Shoes

❋ It is always hard to understand the pain another person feels unless you have walked a mile in that person's shoes.

❋ Have the C/A write what they feel the statement "walk a mile in another person's shoes" means. Have the girls collaborate about what they have written. Discuss how they think they would feel in someone else's shoes.

❋ Now discuss the components of empathy as it relates to this activity. As the girls begin to understand empathy, empower them to take a stand when they see someone being victimized by relational aggression.

STRATEGY 31

"It's Her Story"

❀ Have the girl think of someone she knows who has been the victim of RA. Have her write a story about the victim using the outline below.

Chapter 1 ....What do you think of her?

Chapter 2 ....Why do you think she is a victim?

Chapter 3 ....If nothing changes, how will her story end?

Chapter 4 ....What could you do to help her?

How could you contribute to her situation in a positive way?

(Make this suggestion a reality!)

Chapter 5 ....Now how will her story end?

"Life is a Party... and Everyone is Invited"

❀ We're throwing a party and need a guest list. Have the girl create her personal guest list for her party while thinking of these questions:

- What attracts you to your guests?
- Why would you invite someone to be your guest at a party?
- What qualities would he/she have?
- Would you be on his/her guest list?

❀ Discuss the qualities that attract us to others and the positives and negatives of having different personality traits. Help girls to see we don't all have to be alike, enjoy the same things or socialize with each other at all times. However, having one or two close heart friends is a gift you want to give yourself.

"Life is a Party" Part II

On How to Be a Good Hostess...

Everyone has arrived for the party!

❀ In order to be a good hostess, how would you make your guests feel welcome?

❀ List three ways you would make them feel welcome:

❀ How have others made you feel welcome?

❀ What could you do to make others feel included?

❀ What are ways that help you feel included?

❀ Create your own list of strategies to make others feel welcome and included in class, during lunch, in the halls, after school, at sporting events, etc.

❀ Discuss the etiquette of being a good hostess.

Make Some Magic

❋ Using Model Magic instruct the C/A to create a symbol that represents how she sees herself. We suggest using white Model Magic so the C/A will not associate a feeling with a particular color. As she is working with the model magic explore with her feelings she may have surrounding relational aggression and incidences she may have been involved in.

❋ Empower the C/A by using what she has designed as a metaphor for the magical ability she has to change the "shape" of her image. The Model Magic™ can be painted with a color of her choosing after it has been created.

The Feeling Dictionary

✿ It is important to give C/A an accurate way to express the emotions she is feeling. Instruct the C/A to use a dictionary to look up and write down the definitions of feeling words. Have her separate the feeling words into either pleasant or unpleasant depending on what these feelings elicit. Allow her to begin with feeling words that she has experienced. Continue to add to this list. Discuss with the girl the true meaning of the words she has chosen and determine if her definition is different than the dictionary. Encourage her to use these words with others when expressing how she feels.

Intensity of Feelings	HAPPY	SAD	ANGRY	CONFUSED
HIGH	Elated Excited Overjoyed Thrilled Exuberant Ecstatic Delighted	Depressed Disappointed Alone Hurt Left out Dejected Hopeless Sorrowful Crushed	Furious Enraged Outraged Aggravated Irate Seething	Bewildered Trapped Troubled Desperate Lost
MEDIUM	Cheerful Up Good Relieved Satisfied Contented	Heartbroken Down Upset Distressed Regret	Upset Mad Annoyed Frustrated Agitated Hot Disgusted	Disorganized Foggy Misplaced Disoriented Mixed up
MILD	Glad Content Satisfied Pleasant Fine Mellow Pleased	Unhappy Moody Blue Sorry Lost Bad Dissatisfied	Perturbed Uptight Dismayed Put out Irritated Touchy	Unsure Puzzled Bothered Uncomfortable Undecided Baffled Perplexed

The Feeling Dictionary

Intensity of Feelings	AFRAID	WEAK	STRONG	GUILTY
HIGH	Terrified Horrified Scared stiff Petrified Fearful Panicky	Helpless Hopeless Beat Overwhelmed Small Exhausted Drained	Powerful Aggressive Gung ho Potent Super Forceful Proud Determined	Sorrowful Remorseful Ashamed Unworthy Worthless
MEDIUM	Scared Frightened Threatened Insecure Uneasy Shocked	Dependent Incapable Lifeless Tired Rundown Lazy Insecure Shy	Energetic Capable Confident Persuasive Sure	Sorry Lowdown Sneaky
MILD	Apprehensive Nervous Worried Timid Unsure Anxious	Unsatisfied Under par Shaky Unsure Soft Lethargic Inadequate	Secure Durable Adequate Able Capable	Embarrassed

Source Unknown

101½

Creative

Strategies
and Activities
for Working
with
Relational
Aggression

Strategies 36-53
*Classroom or Small
Group Activities*

Bullying can happen in a very subtle manner and the teacher may be unaware, but the effect can be just as serious as an overt physical attack. It may be a mumbled threat, a passed note or just a look, but the victim may be significantly distressed by it and be unable to concentrate on the lesson

However vigilant a teacher is, it is impossible to prevent all bullying by relying on supervision alone. Teachers must create a classroom environment in which bullying is unacceptable and is openly discussed with the students. If an incident of bullying does occur in a classroom, the students need to know how a teacher will react if they decide to speak out. The students must feel confident that their concerns will be dealt with calmly and fairly.

Using regular classroom meetings is crucial in the continued educational process of RA and all types of bullying. Teachers can use a number of strategies to implement this into the class curriculum.

Zone Mapping

❀ Overview:

Mapping will provide an opportunity to identify areas of your school where students feel more vulnerable.

❀ Materials Needed:

- 11x14 piece of paper
- Pens, colored pencils, crayons or markers

❀ Procedure:

Have the students draw a map of the school (can be a simple rectangle with the landmarks drawn in), then have the students use colored markers/crayons to identify the areas in which the bullying may take place (ie red=unsafe territory, green=no problems, blue= ok, but some concerns, etc.)

❀ Follow Up:

There are "zones" in every school that students avoid because they feel uncomfortable. Identifying theses zones will help when making a plan for avoiding the "zones" and finding a new way of getting around school.

Explore with the students different ideas to improve the "zones" in their school. This strategy will also provide school personnel with a means to discover possible areas where increased supervision may be necessary.

STRATEGY 37

Garbage In / Garbage Out

❁ Overview:

We have all done or said things we wish we had not. We may say things we do not mean, exclude someone from the group, or stand by and laugh as someone is being picked on.

❁ Materials Needed:

• Garbage In / Garbage Out Worksheet
• Pens, pencils

❁ Procedure:

Have C/A list on the garbage can worksheet things they want to throw away (attitudes, behaviors, or certain situations). They can throw away regrets they may have or feelings related to being hurt by others.

❁ Follow Up:

• Help them identify why they would throw these things away.
• Explore how they would respond differently if they had an opportunity to do so.
• List three ways they could make better choices in the future.

Garbage In/Garbage Out

Directions: On the lines below, list attitudes, behaviors or situations that you would like to throw away.

S T R A T E G Y   3 8

All the World's a Stage

❀ Overview:

Exploring the "Star Power" each child/adolescent has within them!

❀ Materials Needed:

- All the World's a Stage worksheet
- Pens, colored pencils, crayons or markers

❀ Procedure:

Ask C/A's to imagine they are movie stars. Ask, "what would your starring role be," and in what kind of movie (drama, horror, comedy, etc.). Ask the C/A's to give their movie a title and setting, then have them share their movie with the group.

Encourage the C/A's to think outside the box. Encourage them to explore the possibilities of their future.

❀ Discussion Questions:

- Is the character similar to who they are or does it represent them in an alternate way?
- Why did they choose to portray themselves that way?
- Was it a positive or negative portrayal?
- How could they learn from this character?
- Would they invite anyone else to be on stage with them?
- Why this particular person?

❀ Follow Up:

- Explore with the C/A how they have portrayed themselves.
- List four "Star" qualities they discovered about themselves through this activity.

All the World's a Stage

Directions: On the lines below, answer the following questions.

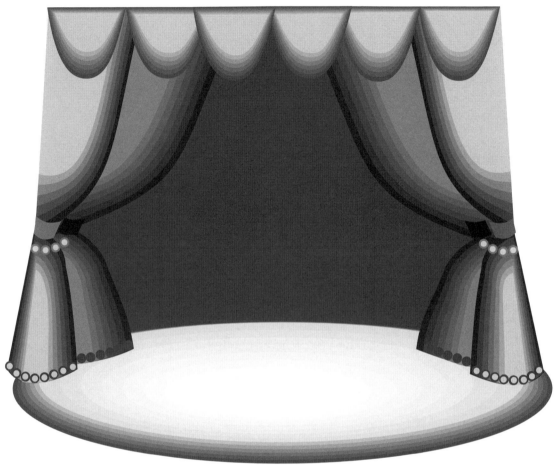

What would your starring role be? _____

What kind of movie would it be? Why? _____

_____

What would the title of your movie be? _____

_____

Briefly describe what your movie would be about: _____

"We're All in This Together"

❀ Overview:

It helps to know there is someone there during the tough times.

❀ Materials Needed:

- "We're All in This Together" worksheet
- Pens, pencils, colored markers

❀ Procedure:

Ask the C/A's what they think this statement means: "We're all in this together." Using the boat worksheet have them write what they think they have in common with each other (we all like music or we all like to go to the movies, etc…).

❀ Follow Up:

After they have finished with their boats, tape them together in a row to represent how they can bond together to help each other cope through some of their common issues.

Then have them share struggles they may have in common (we have all had our feelings hurt, we all feel left out at times …) Share that we all have common struggles, but when we work together, it is easier to cope and not feel alone.

Knowing someone is *there* for you will help you feel stronger!

"We're All in This Together"

Directions: Write words on the sail of the boat to describe what you think you have in common with other girls.

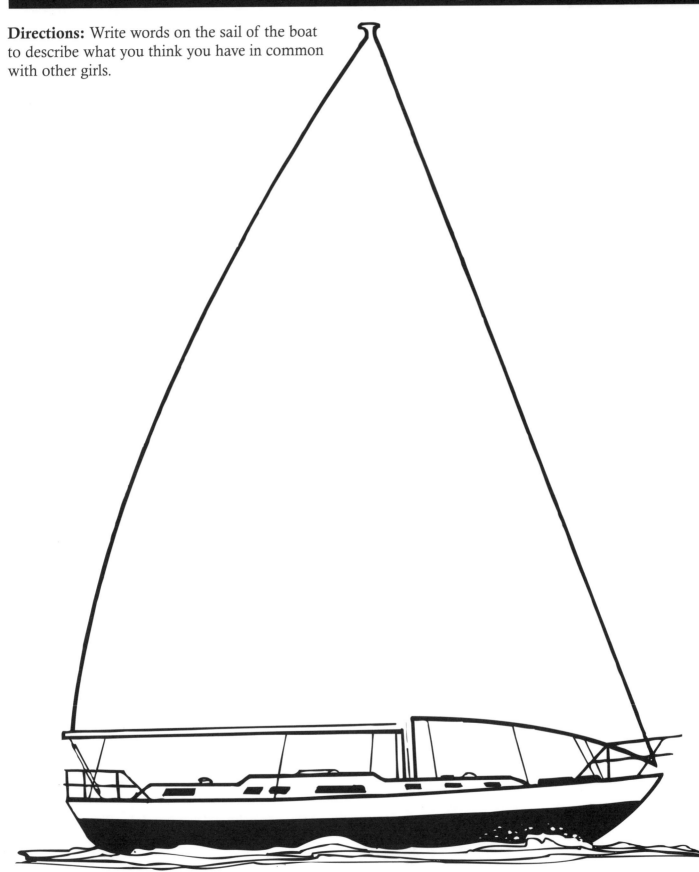

STRATEGY 40

It's not **MY** *problem...or is it?*

❀ Give each C/A a blank piece of paper and have them write down one problem they are currently dealing with. Inform them not to put their names, another person's name, or any other identifying information on the paper.

❀ Then hand the sheets back to the leader. The leader will read the problems and ask the girls to discuss how to solve or cope with each problem (discourage any discussions about whose problem they think they may be discussing, anonymity is key here).

❀ Discuss how this activity made each of them feel. Did they feel a sense of connection knowing their problems are shared by others?

STRATEGY 41

Is the Grass Greener on the Other Side?

❀ Explore with group members what they think the statement "the grass is always greener on the other side" means.

❀ Discuss why people try to change to fit in because they think 'the other side" is better than who they are.

❀ Discuss that although someone may appear to "have it all," they may be dealing with their own issues or problems as well.

❀ Have the girls give you a dictionary definition of the word content.

❀ Then have them list three reasons to be content with who they are.

Ramblin' Road Trip Part 1

❀ Overview:

Identify characteristics that will help girls overcome obstacles.

❀ Materials Needed:

- Ramblin' Road Trip Worksheet
- Pens, pencils, colored markers

❀ Procedure:

Divide the girls into groups of 4-6 members. Hand out the Ramblin' Road Trip worksheet. Tell each group they are going on a trip. They must each put one item into the suitcase that they will NEED on the trip as described in the directions on the worksheet.

❀ Discussion:

- Have each group share what they decided to bring on their trip.
- How are the items in the suitcase going to help them on their journey?
- How could these items help them through their everyday life?
- Did anyone emerge as the leader or "travel guide" during the discussion?

❀ Follow up:

Discuss how they determined which items they would bring. Help the group understand that the journey can be more empowering when traveled together. On this journey of life, remind girls that they have the power to unite and overcome the obstacles of relational aggression.

Ramblin' Road Trip

❀ **Directions:** You and your friends are going on a trip. Get your suitcase ready! Choose wisely, you and your friends can only bring one item each that will help you overcome obstacles such as gossip, exclusion or teasing. The items you bring could be a trait such as your sense of humor, kindness or compassion. Just remember to bring those things that will help you through everyday life. Write these items on the lines below.

A Picture is Worth a Thousand Words

❁ Show two pictures depicting what could be interpreted as relational aggression and one depicting healthy behavior between girls. (You can do an internet search for these images.)

❁ Ask the girls to share what they think is being depicted in each picture. There is no right or wrong interpretation. Based on the different interpretations from the group, explore with the girls the idea that there is usually more to a situation than meets the eye.

❁ Explain to them that this is often how rumors and gossip get started. Tell them to remember to STOP and think that what they see is not always the whole story, so don't judge others.

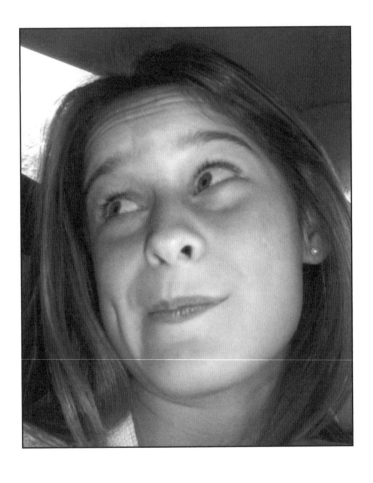

A Sweet Suite

❀ Overview:

Help girls focus on the needs and feelings of others.

❀ Materials Needed:

• A Sweet Suite Worksheet
• Pens, pencils, colored markers, crayons

❀ Procedure:

Randomly select one girl in each group. Inform the girls that today they are going to create a "sweet suite" for the selected person. As the worksheet is circulated around, each person is to draw or write something positive in this person's "suite" that they think would make the selected girl feel happy, comfortable, relaxed, safe, etc.

As each person adds something to the room, they are to describe what they are drawing and why they are adding it to the room.

Repeat this exercise until all the girls have their very own suite.

❀ Follow up:

• Explore with the girls how they decided what to put in the suite.
• How did they feel showing they cared for someone else?
• Encourage the girls to think of others and challenge them to show others that they care.
• Have the girls list three ways they can show a peer that they care.

A Sweet Suite

❀ **Directions:** Draw a picture or write words describing something positive in this suite.

STRATEGY 45

~~~~~~

Life Swap

❋ Have the girls discuss what it would be like to change their personality. Tell them to pick a different personality trait to swap with another person. Discuss the personality swap and the benefits of the new trait they have chosen. Explore with the girls the different ways to incorporate this new trait into their everyday life. This activity can help the girls to recognize their potential for change.

STRATEGY 46

~~~~~~

Is it Okay?

❋ **Overview:**

Many times we do things even when we know they are wrong.

❋ **Materials Needed:**

- "Is it Okay?" Worksheet
- Pens or pencils

❋ **Procedure:**

Ask the girls to complete the worksheets without putting their names on them. After collecting everyone's worksheet, discuss their responses together.

❋ **Follow up:**

Discuss with the girls the different situations listed on the worksheet, "Is it Okay?". Help them identify their normative beliefs. Help them see that we do things even though we know it is not right. Challenge them to ask themselves why they do things they know they should not do. Brainstorm ideas to help them make better choices and challenge old behaviors.

~~~~~~~~~~~~~~~~~~~~~~~~~~~~ 85 ~~~~~~~~~~~~~~~~~~~~~~~~~~~~

Is it Okay?

Answer the following by circling the appropriate number. 1=you rarely do this and 6=you do this often.

How often do you...

	Rarely..........Sometimes.............Often					
Spread rumors	1	2	3	4	5	6
Share with someone a secret your friend told you	1	2	3	4	5	6
Talk on the internet about someone	1	2	3	4	5	6
Roll your eyes when someone walks by	1	2	3	4	5	6
Whisper in front of someone	1	2	3	4	5	6
Pick on someone for what they are wearing or how they look	1	2	3	4	5	6
Exclude someone from being in your group	1	2	3	4	5	6
Threaten not to play/spend time with someone	1	2	3	4	5	6
Take a (crayon, marker, CD, someone else's property) that is not yours	1	2	3	4	5	6
Ignore someone if he/she approaches you	1	2	3	4	5	6

STRATEGY 47

Stair Steps

❀ Overview:

There are times we have inappropriate expectations of people in our lives. This activity will help in identifying appropriate expectations of people.

❀ Materials Needed:

- Stair Steps Worksheet
- Pens or pencils

❀ Procedure:

Using the Stair Step worksheet, ask the C/A's, what they would expect from a stranger, an acquaintance, a friend, and a best friend.

Guided by the professional, have the C/A's brainstorm expectations they would have of each role represented by the people on each step. For example, you would have NO expectations from a relationship with a stranger. However, you would expect mild courtesy from an acquaintance and trust or loyalty from your best friend.

❀ Follow up:

Discuss with the C/A the importance of having appropriate role expectations for the people in their lives. Explain that you shouldn't expect best friend behavior from an acquaintance, or friend behavior from a stranger. Share how this activity can help them begin to have a clear framework for appropriate role expectations.

Stair Steps

Directions: Below the step, list expectations you would have of each person.

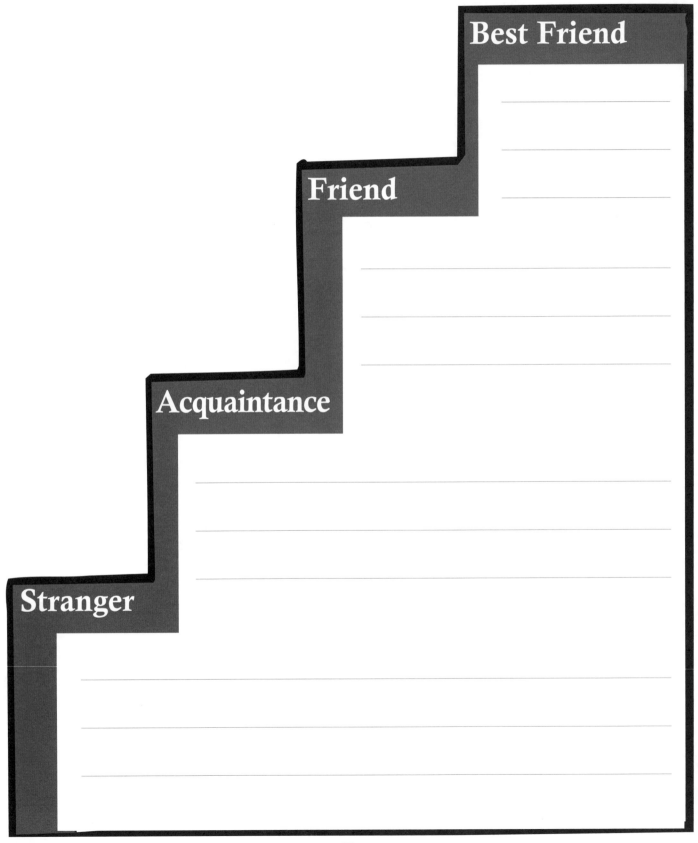

S T R A T E G Y   4 8

Calendar of Caring

❈ For each of the twelve months have the students create a calendar that focuses on what they can do for others. They may want to choose a character word for each month, such as respect and then decide how they can show respect for others during that month.

❈ List at least four suggestions to cover each week of the month. At the end of the month have them share with you the different ways they were able to show someone they care. You may want to have a reward or recognition for the girl or girls who were the most creative in the ways they showed someone they cared.

Drama Squad: Act It Out

✦ Overview:

We all behave and react to situations in ways we wish we did not.
Learn a new way to respond to relationally aggressive situations.

✦ Materials Needed:

• "Role Play" worksheet on the following page
• Spacious area for role playing

✦ Procedure:

Girls will act out RA situations (i.e. gossip, exclusion) and suggest alternative ways to deal with each.

Have the girls create a skit depicting different RA situations. The girls may need a jump start in creating their skits. A scenario suggestion would be for the girls to portray how they see other girls treating each other at school. After the role play have the girls review the basic theme of the skit. Then discuss the following:

• Describe each of the characters in the skit.
• Describe the feelings of each of the characters.
• What was the problem or conflict?

After the discussion, have the girls recreate the skit with a new ending using a positive outcome. Now discuss the following:

• How was this conflict resolved?
• What are some other ways this situation could have been resolved?
• How can you apply this to a situation you have experienced?

✦ Follow up:

Using the skits they have created, discuss with the girls the difference between the original and the new ending. Discuss why girls do not automatically use the positive outcome in everyday situations. How will they begin to apply the new way of handling RA situations?

Role Play Guidelines

❀ 3-4 girls per skit.

❀ List the characters and their relationship with each other.

❀ Keep the skits brief (2-3 minutes).

❀ Have a beginning and an end.

❀ Title the skit.

Skit details using outline above:

"Link it Up"

❀ Overview:

Girls are stronger "linked" together than they are alone.

❀ Materials Needed:

• "Link it Up" worksheet

• Pens, pencils, colored markers, crayons

❀ Procedure:

Using the "Link it Up" worksheet, have the girls write in positive or strong characteristics about themselves on one of the chain links. Then display all as a "chain link" or connected links on a wall.

❀ Follow up:

Once linked together discuss the concept of "strength in numbers" and the power they have when they put all of their positive qualities together. Educate girls that a strong sisterhood built on positive strengths can combat just about ANYTHING!

"Link it Up"

❋ **Directions:** List a positive characteristic about yourself on each link.

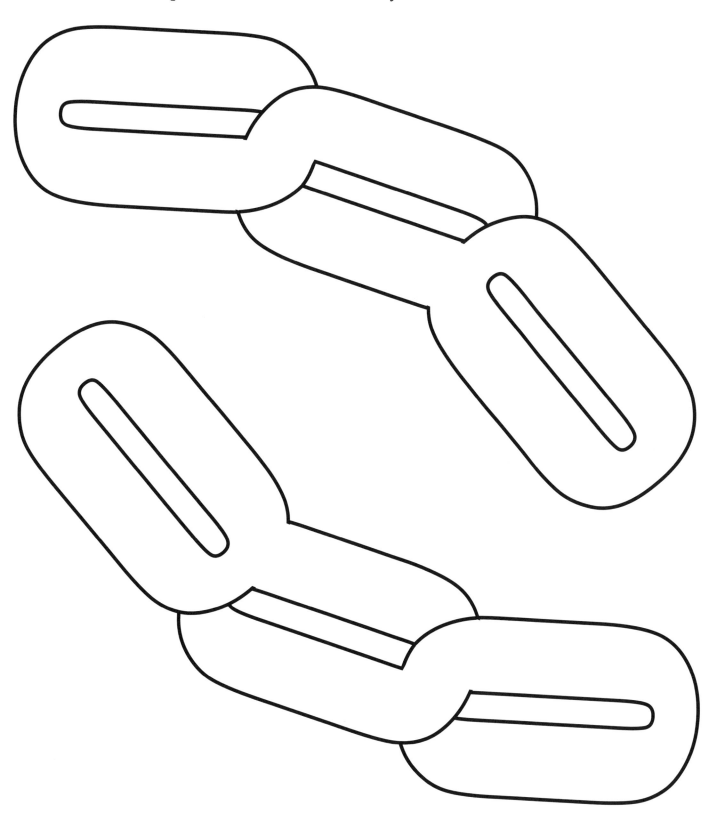

"Rick the Pumpkin"

❋ This is an activity to emphasize the component of empathy. Each C/A is sent home with an item (i.e. an egg, small pumpkin, bag of flour, etc...) to keep for one week. They are responsible for caring for this item as if it were their child. They should name it, feed it, bathe it, read to it, take care of it and nurture it as a child. They must bring it to school everyday and take it with them wherever they go.

❋ Explore with the C/A's how it feels to care for someone else. Discuss with them the idea of nurturing, caring and showing empathy for others.

❋ This is a great exercise in life skills also, so you may want to consider having the social studies teacher work with you on this project as a grade for the C/A's.

Proverbs

❀ Using the beginning of the proverbs, have the C/A's complete what they think the ending would be. Discuss with the C/A's words of wisdom and their meaning. Reflect with the C/A's about the choices they make and the outcomes they may have.

Never underestimate the power of....

You can lead a horse to water but.....

Don't bite the hand that....

No news is....

If you lie with dogs, you'll...

An idle mind....

Where there's smoke there's.....

Two's Company, Three's.....

If at first you don't succeed.....

You get out of something what you.....

The A.C.T. Approach

❀ Overview:

Give the girls positive, practical approaches to change. This will help them stay focused on making better choices.

❀ Materials Needed:

• The A.C.T. Worksheet
• Pen, pencil, colored pencils, colored markers, crayons

❀ Procedure:

Using the A.C.T worksheet on the next page, brainstorm other acronyms to help implement ideas for change. When the "brainstorming" is complete, create posters using these sayings and post them in the classroom and in the halls of the school.

❀ Follow up:

Discuss with the C/A or group the power of the mind. They have the power to CHOOSE to A.C.T. differently. In choosing a more positive behavior, they can truly become empowered young women and change the sometimes hurtful dynamics that occur. Explore with the girls specific situations when and where the A.C.T. approach can be applied.

The A.C.T. Approach

❋ **Directions:** In the blank boxes, create positive words using the A.C.T. acronym.

Choose How You

Assert

Compassion

Truthfully

A

C

T

A

C

T

Always

Control your

Tongue

Always

Control your

Texting

A

C

T

101½ *Creative*
Strategies and Activities for Working with Relational Aggression

Strategies 54-80
School Interventions

It all starts with a school-wide commitment to end relational aggression. From there an effective approach focuses on changing classroom climates and addressing RA with individual girls. It is important to note that success comes with sustained programs that teach tolerance and always keep RA in the fore front of everyone's mind.

In order to be successful, it is important for the school to have very clear limits regarding unacceptable behavior, and to make it a positive place where caring and pro-social behavior is encouraged and relational aggression is firmly discouraged.

Remember, for your school to be successful in combating all forms of relational aggression the following suggestions must be shared with all faculty and staff. Don't forget to include the cafeteria staff, custodians, community volunteers and parents.

STRATEGY 54

Use the Relational Aggression Survey

❋ Conduct an assessment using the Relational Aggression Survey from Strategy 1 (page 19).

❋ Compile the information to identify specific RA dynamics in your school.

❋ During a staff meeting or the school in-service day, share the survey results with ALL faculty and staff including the cafeteria staff, maintenance personnel, and anyone who comes in contact with C/A's.

❋ Determine what action steps you will begin to take based on the information you learned from the surveys.

STRATEGY 55

Keep A High Profile!

❋ All forms of bullying including relational aggression thrive on secrecy. Therefore, the more publicity the better! Address RA in as many publications and posters as possible.

❋ Some ideas are:
  • Brochures - to all parents
  • Handbook - a clear statement addressing the school-wide policies
  • Posters displayed around the school
  • Newsletters
  • School news program

STRATEGY 56

Observation Deck

❋ Make your presence known! RA is sneaky and likes to go undetected, meaning that it's taking place when adults aren't watching. If you have completed strategy 36 with your C/A's, then you have identified zones where RA may be occurring. However, we know that it lurks in the hallways, lunch areas, bathrooms and playgrounds. So really observe C/A interactions, don't just stand by and watch.

STRATEGY 57

Hang Time

❋ Find a way to "hang out" with students. For example, sit with them at lunch, stand outside your class during class change, invite a few to "hang out" with you during your planning period, after school or at sporting events. Research what's popular today such as music, movies, fashion, latest video games, etc...in order to have topics to discuss with them in their world. Being prepared will make for less awkward moments.

STRATEGY 58

Classroom Connection

❋ Each week take 30 minutes of classroom time to connect with C/A's in an informal way about personal issues, what's going on in their lives, and discussing topics of their choice, all academics aside. Facilitate discussions about clips from movies (show clips if possible), lyrics from songs or situations you have seen taking place at your school. If it is a topic you feel they will not share openly or honestly, have them write their comments and share anonymously.

S T R A T E G Y   5 9

Classroom Clips

❋ Use banners or posters displaying a definition of RA and the behaviors that are not tolerated. Also display the positive behaviors to replace them. Have students decorate other banners and posters with positive messages about friendships and how to treat others. Allow the students to take pictures of themselves and their friends to display with notes about positive traits that their friends have. It is important to ensure that all students are included.

S T R A T E G Y   6 0

Class Rules

❋ At the beginning of the school year leave one bulletin board blank. Within the first week of school, develop an Anti-RA bulletin board with the class setting the rules and having input for any consequences for breaking the rules. Refer to the bulletin board as needed. You may want to select a different student each week to read the rules to the class.

S T R A T E G Y   6 1

Community Connections 1

❋ Identify community volunteers and organizations. Provide training and education concerning the issues surrounding RA. Use these volunteers to raise awareness as well as offer their time to create a nurturing and supportive environment. By utilizing outside resources, you bring a new perspective and opportunities for students to connect with other adults. Possible organizations to partner with include: local law enforcement, civic groups, community mentoring programs, etc.

STRATEGY 62

Community Connections 2

❁ Utilizing volunteers or professionals from the community, have them read stories to elementary school students about RA, and to spend time discussing RA issues. Use elementary scenario's to demonstrate RA at their age level.

In middle school, use the volunteers as mentors to cultivate relationships with groups of girls. One activity would be to watch the movie "Mean Girls" (this movie is rated PG-13, parental consent is advised). Discuss the movie in terms of their girl culture and perceptions.

In high school the volunteers could empower and teach students ways to utilize their individual talents and gifts to be used in the community through giving back as volunteers with younger age girls. The volunteers could help coordinate a service learning project for the girls to be involved with. Connect with a local college for potential mentors to work with high school girls.

STRATEGY 63

Parental Awareness

❁ Develop pamphlets and brochures to distribute during parent/teacher conferences or PTO meetings to educate parents about the policies and procedures concerning school bullying and relational aggression. Share with parent's information about RA to increase awareness and help address RA in the home environment. Consider hosting parent workshops or community-wide events to provide in depth training about RA.

STRATEGY 64

Keep it Real Teachers

❋ Let's not forget that RA happens among adults. As teachers, counselors, social workers, and administrators, students are watching you and your behavior. If you are whispering about other teachers or staff and the students hear you then you are teaching them it is okay to gossip or talk about others. Watch your own actions towards others. You are a role-model.

STRATEGY 65

Parent and Student Task Force

❋ Ask for volunteers to be a part of this task force. The purpose is to gain an understanding of RA and how it affects their school. Discuss and develop ways to combat RA in their schools and in their communities. Have the parents and students take turns sharing information about RA and how they have experienced its affects. Are they similar or different? Brainstorm ways to confront RA appropriately.

STRATEGY 66

Anti-RA Day / Week

❋ Hopefully your school will allow for a full week for RA education and awareness. Kick off this week by announcing the upcoming events. Ideas can include an essay writing contest, poster or banner contest, song writing contest, poetry contest or drama skit performance. Choose a theme and a color to represent Anti-RA Education week/day. Each day of the week have something fun planned relating to RA. To be most successful remember to include the girls in the planning of this day/week. Encourage the faculty and staff to participate in all the activities as well.

Random Acts of Kindness

RAK 'EM UP!!

❋ Implement a school-wide praise reward system to "catch a kid" doing something kind. All school personnel should be involved in "catching a kid," from the principal to the teachers, to the support staff and everyone in between. This system is based on cumulative points to be tracked by the homeroom teacher. Age appropriate rewards will be given either on a weekly or bi-weekly basis. Some rewards should be connected to their academics. For example the reward could be a free homework pass to be used at the child's discretion, or possibly two to three points added to a test score or homework grade. A fun reward could be movie tickets or gift certificates to a discount store or your local toy store. Many organizations will donate these items to your school. Speak to the local manager.

Elementary RAK 'EM UP!! Cards

Building on strategy 67 this activity helps students get started spreading random acts of kindness. The activity has been divided into specific cards for Elementary, Middle and High school. You can photocopy these reproducible cards on card stock, cut them out and give them to the students. Encourage them to make a plan how to complete the act of kindness and then report back to you what they experienced. There are also blank cards for your own creative ideas.

Choose not to engage in gossip	Draw someone a kind picture
Invite someone to play with you	Let someone borrow your crayons or markers
Give someone a nice compliment	Smile at someone you don't play with
Help the teacher	Don't laugh if someone falls down
Help someone cut and paste	Choose not to spread gossip
Help someone in a wheelchair	Spread some nice news about someone
If someone falls down on the playground, help them up	Apologize if you accidentally hurt someone
Talk to the new student in your class	

Middle School RAK 'EM UP!! Cards

Photocopy these reproducible cards onto card stock, cut them out and give them to the students. Encourage them to make a plan how to complete the act of kindness and then report back to you what they experienced. There are also blank cards for your own creative ideas.

Choose not to engage in gossip	Sit with someone different at lunch
Invite someone to hang out with you	Let someone borrow your clothes
Give someone a nice compliment	Smile at someone you don't know at school
Volunteer to tutor another student	Apologize if you accidentally hurt someone
Help someone with a problem	Talk with a new student in your class
Help someone roll their wheelchair	Challenge yourself for one day to talk with someone you do not know
Send an encouraging text message to another student	Post a nice comment on someone's message board

High School RAK 'EM UP!! Cards

Photocopy these reproducible cards on card stock, cut them out and give them to the students.
Encourage them to make a plan how to complete the act of kindness and then report back to you
what they experienced. There are also blank cards for your own creative ideas.

Volunteer as a mentor to a younger student	Give someone who is not in your group a kind glance
Write someone a nice note	Invite someone new to a party
Give someone a compliment	Ask someone new about their interests
Say Hi to someone you don't hang out with	Send an encouraging text message
Invite someone outside your social group to lunch	If you hear gossip, choose not to spread it
Ask someone about their day or weekend	Help someone with a problem
Post a nice message on a message board	

S T R A T E G Y   6 9

Round Table Discussions

❀ Every two weeks, have pizza with a group of girls. This can be a focus group to help you stay in touch with your students, celebrate achievements, or recognize good behaviors. This can be an opportunity for the students in the group to participate in a solution-focused discussion designed to alleviate school aggression, violence or other issues concerning them. Consider inviting the principal or other personnel to participate.

S T R A T E G Y   7 0

"Coffee Talk"

❀ One of the latest fads with our girls is drinking coffee. Find a time to have "Coffee Talk." Brew a pot of coffee, pick a topic and talk it up with the girls about what is going on in their world. Have the girls contribute to helping each other solve what may be concerning them. Many times girls need a jumpstart question. You could start with asking them how they see other girls treating each other and how they could contribute to changing that.

❀ If you want to be really creative, have the girls create a "coffee house." You could have volunteers provide drinks, snacks, etc. The girls could expand their "coffee talk" to include poetry readings, music, or special guest speakers. Let the girls decide how they want their coffee house to be.

STRATEGY 71

Cyber Awareness

❋ Take time to educate yourself about the technological way girls use the internet to harass, intimidate and bully each other. Becoming e-savvy will help you stay on top of the how C/A's use the internet to communicate and stay in touch with their friends. Use the information from the Cyber-Bullying section at the beginning of this book. Also consider inviting a computer safety expert to come and speak to the school.

STRATEGY 72

Adult Mentors

❋ Use adult volunteers as mentors. Teach the volunteers about RA and encourage them to be available for C/A to talk to if needed. These wonderful volunteers can also help with developing and or implementing Anti-RA day. Mentors provide positive support, role modeling and practical suggestions for girls needing someone to talk to. During mentor training discuss the importance of confidentiality and the responsibilities of being a mentor. Adult mentors focus on the individual student rather than a group.

Perception or Reality?

❋ Do an internet search for optical illusions. Choose a picture for the girls to look at. After they have pondered for awhile and there has been discussion about the picture point out to them that the way we each see things is not always the same. Our perception is *our* reality. There are times when we will not always agree with our friends or see things eye to eye, but we can still be friends. It is okay for us to all be different and see things differently.

To the professional, it is important to note that girls react differently to different types of relational aggression based on their perception of how they are being treated. We must address RA from their perspective in order to help them cope more effectively.

This is a picture of a face, but it is also the word "LIAR."

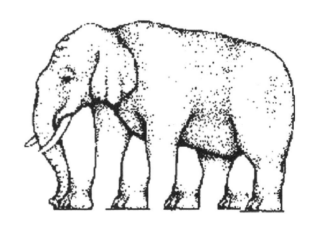

Can you count the legs on this elephant?

Source: Unknown

"StarBucks"

❋ As adults we get caught up at times using gender phrases for our girls. For example we say "be nice" or "little girls don't act like that," yet we fail to provide girls with the appropriate behavior we would like them to display.

To promote "star" behavior, we must teach what is acceptable and appropriate. Using bulletin boards or other displays, decorate stars with words or phrases that are positive behaviors. For example, sharing, saying kind words, etc…then, when you see a girl displaying the acceptable behavior, reward her with a "StarBuck." When she has accumulated a certain number of stars she can use them to "buy" or exchange for a reward.

Pass the Gossip Please?

❋ Have the girls sit in a circle. You are going to whisper a message into the ear of the person to your right (this can be any phrase or word you want it to be). You can only say it once and then they are to whisper the message, or what they think they heard, into the ear of the next person, continuing around the circle until it gets back to you.

• How did the original message change?

• How far from the truth was the ending message from the original?

Ask, "what usually happens when a story gets passed form one person to another?" The story changes! The more people tell the story, the more it changes. This is just like gossip. When gossip starts it usually changes as the story is told and turns out not to be true. Don't always believe what you hear! It may not be true!

Cheerleader Power

❀ Cheerleaders have always been popular; however, they are popular, sometimes for good and sometimes for not so good reasons. Talk with the cheerleader coach and ask for her/his help with this strategy.

❀ Ask the cheerleader's why they think they are popular? Explore with them what a role model is and ask them if they think they are role models. After some discussion, ask them to try for one day being totally aware that they are role models. Will it change their behavior, will they do things differently or treat people differently?

❀ Have the cheerleader coach point out positive behaviors she notices and reward those who display "positive cheerleader power." If appropriate, use the high school cheerleaders to help promote anti-RA behavior at the middle and elementary schools. Also, encourage them to come up with a cheer they can do on anti-RA day

The Good News Book

❀ Have a centrally located notebook that is like a guestbook but designated for the staff to write positive comments about each other and the C/A's. Take time every day to read what your colleagues have to say about each other. Compliment the person on what you have read. In addition, if you see a positive comment about a C/A, compliment that C/A. This gives everyone the chance to receive a validating compliment and to learn how to give them as well.

STRATEGY 78

Braggin' Board

❋ Have a Braggin' Board displayed for the staff to brag about each other. They can share pictures, awards, or any other information to recognize their achievements. Please be sure you have permission from the peer you want to brag about before posting any information about him/her. This is designed to keep morale high and attention focused on the positive achievements of others. Contact the local newspaper if some achievements are unique and newsworthy.

STRATEGY 79

Note Worthy News

❋ Every school sends out newsletters relaying information concerning the school. While good news is relayed here it is often in a small box along with all of the other news. Instead have a separate newsletter for ONLY good news. All parents love to read good news about their children. Feature several students in each edition throughout the year.

STRATEGY 80

Hot Spots

❋ This is a fun yet insightful activity to be done at staff meetings. Have the faculty and staff create a map of the school and identify what they consider to be the hot spots for RA/bullying. Then have the staff compare their map with those of the students if you had students complete strategy 36.

❋ Compare the different maps from the students and staff and see if they match. It may be that there are a few spots that the staff are unaware of or surprised by. If new hot spots are discovered, brainstorm how to increase supervision in these areas. The school may want to assign color codes to certain areas. For instance, the red zone would be a high alert area and require increased supervision.

101½ Creative Strategies and Activities for Working with Relational Aggression

"Shepherding our daughters through adolescence requires that we give them hope, support, safe haven, and, when the time is right, permission to leave us behind; it also requires that we give ourselves permission, in turn, to move on to another stage of life."

Nancy Snyderman- author
Girl in the Mirror: Mothers and Daughters in the Years of Adolescence

Strategies 81-99
Parent Interventions

STRATEGY 81

Speak Her Language

❀ Learn to speak your daughter's language. At times you may feel you and your daughter speak totally different languages. We all want to feel valued and accepted but when we speak different languages we may feel alienated or misunderstood. Take the time to learn how to communicate in a way that speaks unconditional love to your daughter. We recommend T*he Five Love Languages of Children and The Five Love Languages of Teenagers* by Dr. Gary Chapman.

STRATEGY 82

Get Her Involved

❀ Get your daughter involved! Find extracurricular activities outside of school for your daughter to be involved in. This gives her a circle of friends to connect with that may be different from her friends at school and provides her an opportunity to learn more about herself and her talents. Some suggestions are Girl Scouts, Youth Jaycees, recreation leagues and faith based groups.

STRATEGY 83

One for the Team

❀ **TEACH RESPONSIBILITY.**
All members of a team contribute equally for the team to be successful. Your family is a team! Involve your daughter in household responsibilities such as unloading the dishwasher, taking the trash out, feeding the family pet, keeping her room clean, etc... You may be met with opposition in the beginning; however, in the end you will see a responsible young adult emerge who contributes not only to her "home" team but also to her community and society.

STRATEGY 84

Connecting

❋ Find an adult mentor who can be an encourager and someone your daughter can connect with and share her feelings. As parents we like to think that our girls will come to us and talk about anything; however, the reality is that they may not. Find someone you trust with your daughter and encourage a relationship that builds trust and openness. Remember, this is not someone to take your place, but someone you trust who will guide her and accept her. The school counselor could help you find a mentor and provide more information about mentoring.

STRATEGY 85

What's your Talent?

❋ Use YOUR Talent. We all have a unique talent that can be utilized. Volunteer at your daughter's school. Schools always need volunteers to help in a myriad of different ways. Inquire with your daughter's teacher or office staff as to how they could best utilize you. If you have nursing skills, assist the school nurse; maybe you love to cook, volunteer in the cafeteria; or your talent might be music, work with the music teacher. There are numerous ways to serve in your child's school.

STRATEGY 86

Be Seen

❋ Make your presence known. Attend open house at the school, attend PTA meetings, schedule a parent teacher conference and discuss not only academically where your daughter stands, but inquire about socially what her teacher may observe as your daughter interacts with her peers. After all, teachers have more opportunities during the day to observe interactions between your daughter and her friends than you do.

STRATEGY 87

Policies and Procedures

❋ Do you know the policies and procedures addressing relational aggression at your daughter's school? It is important that you be educated about the policies and procedures should you ever find your daughter involved in a relationally aggressive situation. Because RA is prevalent in all schools, don't be caught off guard thinking this will not apply to your daughter. Contact the school principal for information about RA and bullying policies and procedures. Consider coordinating a parent night to inform parents of what RA looks like and policies related to RA for the district.

STRATEGY 88

Are you really Available?

❋ Be Available! Listen, don't talk for her. Empathize with your daughter, never minimize what she is going through (her perception is her reality). Words that dismiss how she feels will alienate your relationship. Do not make comments like, "Oh, just ignore them…" or "this really won't be a big deal a week from now." We have two ears and one mouth for a reason… we need to listen twice as much as we speak. The more you listen and refrain from speaking the more often your daughter will open up to you.

STRATEGY 89

You Can't Handle the Truth! Or Can You?

❋ Often your daughter will share if she has been a victim of a situation; however she may not so readily share if she has been the aggressor in the situation. Be open to discuss both sides of the issue with her. Also, watch your reactions to any information your daughter shares with you (shocking or not). You have one chance to make it or break it. If you overreact, she may not be willing to share with you in the future.

STRATEGY 90

She's Watching You!

❊ Be a positive role model. Your daughter is watching you. Teach by example appropriate behaviors in how you should treat others. Talk with her about truly healthy relationships and what true friendships look like. Do not talk about your own friends in a negative way, and do not talk about other children. Look for ways to encourage positive connections and remember that "in order to have a friend, you must be a friend." When she is watching you interact with others she is learning by observing and absorbing everything you do and say. So, be on the alert at all times!

STRATEGY 91

Your own RA experience

❊ Share your own experiences from elementary, middle or high school as it relates to her experience. Whether you were the bully or the victim or somewhere in between, share how you handled relational aggression. Self-disclosure can help your daughter discover her own personal strengths based on your response to the situation. It may be very different or you may find very close similarities. How did you cope in your situation? Explore ways for your daughter to cope and point out the strengths she has to face the situations she may be dealing with.

(Note: Telling her to "just accept it" or "it is just a part of growing up" are not acceptable ways to respond).

STRATEGY 92

Kindness Goes A Long Way

❀ Teach her kindness. Show her small ways in which she can be kind to other people. A kind word goes a long way. Lead by example in ways you show others kindness. Encourage your daughter to send a note to a friend who has been sick, give a simple smile as she passes someone in the hallway or help someone who may be in need. Also, if your daughter has been involved in hurting someone's feelings, have her right a note of apology for what she did.

"No act of Kindness, no matter how small, is ever wasted....." Aesop

STRATEGY 93

Self - Check for Mom

❀ Do a "self- check" of anyone you may have hurt in your past or someone who hurt you. Resolve all bitterness and grudges by apologizing or forgiving those who have hurt you. When you do this, you are teaching your daughter a timeless lesson.

STRATEGY 94

Actions speak louder than words!

❀ Be on the look out! Watch for behavioral changes that are not within the norm for your daughter such as anger, crying, withdrawal from activities, morning or evening anxiety, not wanting to go to school. Any of these may indicate she is struggling with an issue at school. Observe whether these behaviors are unusual, happening more often or happening at certain times. Consult with your school/professional counselor and seek outside counseling if needed.

STRATEGY 95

All About Me! Journal

❋ Encourage your daughter to keep a journal. Have her not only journal incidents of RA but also of her everyday life. Use this for growth and self reflection. Journaling can be very useful in chronic aggressive situations to have documentation of the events. It can also help her express her feelings in an appropriate manner.

STRATEGY 96

All About Her! Journal

❋ Keep your own journal about your daughter's accomplishments. Don't forget to note the positive behaviors that you see. If you begin to have concerns about your daughter's behavior, document these as well. Record any incidences she may be involved in at school related to relational aggression. Document the names of girls involved in the conflict. Keeping a record will help should there be a need for intervention from the school or law enforcement.

STRATEGY 97

Empower Her

❋ Empower your daughter with HER strengths in order to help her feel that she can be strong enough to step up and intervene if she sees a bullying situation or is being bullied. Identify specific strength words to build up and edify your daughter. You can use the following list as a guide.

90 Personal Strength Words

A

____Accepting
____Adventurous
____Appreciative
____Artistic
____Assertive
____Athletic

B

____Bold
____Brave
____Bright

C

____Calm
____Caring
____Cautious
____Clever
____Confident
____Considerate
____Cooperative
____Courageous
____Courteous
____Creative
____Curious

D

____Dedicated
____Dependable
____Dtermined
____Devoted
____Disciplined

E

____Eager
____Efficient
____Encouraging
____Energetic
____Enthusiastic

F

____Fair
____Faithful

____Flexible
____Forgiving
____Friendly
____Fun-Loving

G

____Generous
____Gentle
____Giving
____Good Sport

H

____Hard Worker
____Helpful
____Honest
____Humble
____Humorous

I

____Independent
____Insightful
____Interested
____Involved

L

____Laidback
____Leader
____Likable
____Loving
____Loyal

M

____Mature
____Motivated

N

____Neat
____Nurturing

O

____On Task
____Open-Minded

____Optimistic
____Organized

P

____Patient
____Perceptive
____Persevering
____Positive
____Prepared
____Punctual

Q

____Quiet

R

____Reasonable
____Reliable
____Resourceful
____Respectful

S

____Self-Aware
____Sensitive
____Sharing
____Sincere
____Supportive
____Survivalist

T

____Team Player
____Thoughtful
____Tolerant
____Trustworthy

U

____Understanding
____Unique
____Unselfish

W

____Warm
____Witty

Copied with permission by Bowman & Bowman, *Meaningful Mentoring*

S T R A T E G Y   9 8

Become Techno-Savvy

❁ In this day and time of technology our children are more techno- savvy than most adults. Educate yourself about how they communicate. Cell phones (they are not just for making calls these days), video phones and the internet are all methods children and adolescents use to hurt others. Understanding the technology will help you better track how your child may be bullied or may be bullying others. Ask your child's school counselor for a list of resources.

S T R A T E G Y   9 9

Get Help!!

❁ Many girls will go to their friends for help before they will go to a parent or other trustworthy adult, especially when they reach the teen years. It is important to talk with your daughter about which trustworthy adults she can go to for help.

❁ Complete the following contact sheet with your daughter so she has a list of names to keep with her. By increasing your daughter's support network you increase the chances she will always have someone she can talk to. Also, it is important to know when to seek professional counseling. Consult your school counselor or psychologist for recommendations of therapists in the community who specialize in children and adolescent issues.

Contact Sheet

Write the name of someone you can trust to talk to about the following issues:

Academic problems _____

Problems with a teacher _____

**Another girl being
relationally aggressive toward you** _____

Being picked on while on the bus _____

Harassment in the locker room _____

Witnessing a fight _____

**Someone asks you to "IM"
or email a threat to someone** _____

**A friend tells you
she is going to hurt herself** _____

**A friend tells you she
is going to hurt another girl** _____

**You receive a hateful
email or text message** _____

101½ *Creative* Strategies and Activities for Working with Relational Aggression

This section is devoted to you and is a good reminder of the need to take care of yourself. The more you explore who you are and grow in your own empowerment, the more you can in turn help to empower all of our sisters, young and old.

Kaye & Allyson

Strategies 100-101 1/2
Wrap It Up!!!

Make a W.A.V.E.

❂ Think of two or three women you connect with and ask them to join you in making a commitment to increase their awareness and combat relational aggression. You can create a W.A.V.E. (Women Accepting the Value in Everyone.) A famous comedian once said, "Women could rule the world if they didn't hate each other so much." When women are united through their acceptance of each other's gifts and talents, there is nothing that can't be accomplished.

STRATEGY 101

"You"niquely You

❂ Our girls are all on a journey to define who they are; contributing to that journey is what we hope to do as helpers. On a journey not all roads are defined and there may be major detours and bumps in the road, but by keeping on the right course the destination can be wonderful.

❂ It is in this journey that we see the only difference in human beings is their individuality. As you work with girls to help them define what makes them "You"nique" there are treasures to unfold at every stage. Have your daughter write positive statements about herself on strips of paper. Then find a treasure box at any craft store that she can creatively decorate. Have her place all these positive statements in the treasure box and take one out every day to remind her of her uniqueness and positive qualities.

Just for You!

❋ As a professional, you are also on a journey. Our hope is that we have helped you find fun and exciting ways to lead these young girls. We admire your commitment and dedication in caring for our girls.

❋ We encourage you to take time for yourself by spending more time laughing with your best friend, pampering yourself with a manicure or pedicure, enjoying a massage or facial, taking yoga lessons, learn to dance, etc. Or, be gutsy and go for extreme sports like rock climbing, repelling, scuba diving, snowboarding, white water rafting or whatever you have always wanted to do but never tried. The journey is endless! Just remember, you do so much for others that this one is "Just for You!"

References

Belsey, Bill. "www.cyberbullying.org, "Always on? Always Aware!" available at www.cyberbullying.ca; Internet accessed 8 February 2006.

Brendgen, Mara, Boivin,M., Dionne G., Girard,A., Perusse,D., Vitaro,F.(2005). Examining Genetic and Environmental Effects on Social Aggression. Child Development,76,4.

Chapman, Gary. (1995). *The Five Love Languages*. IL; Northfield Publishing.

Cohen, R.(2002, February).Stop mediating these conflicts now! *The School Mediator: Peer Mediation Insights from the Desk of Richard Cohen.* Electronic newsletter, School Mediation Associates. Retrieved November 30, 2005, from schoolmediation.com

Crick, Nicki R. (1996). The Role of Overt Aggression, Relational Aggression, And Prosocial Behavior In The Prediction Of Children's Future Social Adjustment. Child Development, 67 (5), 2317-2327.

Juvonen, Janna, Nishina,A. (2005). Sticks and Stones May Break My Bones, but Names Will make me Feel Sick: The Psychosocial, Somatic and Scholastic Consequences of Peer Harassment. *Journal of Clinical and Adolescent Psychology*, 34 (1),37-48.

Kowalski, R., Limber, S. P. Scheck, A., Redfearn, M., Allen, J., Calloway, A., Farris, J., Finnegan, K., Keith, M., Kerr, S., Singer, L., Spearman, J., Tripp, L., & Vernon, L. (2005, August). Electronic bullying among school-aged children and youth. Paper presented at the annual meeting of the American Psychological Association. Washington, DC.

Ludwig, Trudy. (2005). *My Secret Bully*. CA; Tricycle Press.

Nelson, David A., Hart, Craig H., Robinson, C. (2005). Relational and Physical Aggression of Preschool Age Children: Peer Status Linkages Across Informants. *Early Education and Development,* 16, (2), 115-140.

Ophelia Project. www.opheliaproject.org

Willard, Nancy. A Parent's guide to Cyberbullying and Cyberthreats. Center for Safe and Responsible Internet Use.

Wiseman, Rosalind. (2002). *Queen Bees and Wannabees.* NY; Crown Publishers.

Ybarra, M. L., & Mitchell, K. J. (2004). Online aggressors/targets, aggressors, and targets: a comparison of associated youth characteristics. *Journal of Child Psychology and Psychiatry*, 45, 1308-1316.

About The Authors

ALLYSON BOWEN

Allyson Bowen, LISW-CP is a Licensed Clinical Social Worker in clinical private practice. She is co-owner and director of Turning Point Counseling in West Columbia, SC. She focuses on motivating teenage girls and educating women of all ages about female relational issues and challenges. Allyson recently developed a Relational Aggression Survey for use in identifying female bullying behaviors in girl's grades 3-12. In addition, Allyson is an adjunct professor in the Social Work Department at a private college focusing on human behavior, sexuality and gender role differences. She has also worked in the medical field and developed a community outreach program for teen mothers.

Allyson's high energy and humor have challenged and motivated participants in making positive changes in their work with youth and adolescents. She is a national consultant and has conducted professional seminars throughout the US and Canada on topics such as relational aggression, anger, and bullying.

Allyson is married to her high school sweetheart and they have one son.

KAYE RANDALL

Kaye Randall, LISW-CP is the very proud mother of a twenty year old daughter, Brianna. This is the role that she cherishes above all others. She is the co-owner and director of Turning Point Counseling in West Columbia, SC. She is a Licensed Clinical Social Worker in private practice. She provides clinical services to children and adolescents in inpatient and outpatient settings. She has extensive experience in bipolar disorder, depression, self-injury and other issues concerning adolescents. In addition, Kaye provides crisis intervention, assessments and counseling services for victims of child abuse and neglect. She works with many children and adolescents who exhibit challenging behaviors such as relational aggression and bullying as well as those who are the victims of these behaviors.

Kaye is co-author of *"See My Pain: Creative Strategies and Activities for Helping Young People Who Self-Injure"* featured in USA Today and *"102 Creative Strategies in Working with Depression."*

Kaye has inspired seminar participants through her practical insights and proactive caring strategies in helping children and adolescents. She has led professional seminars throughout the US and Canada on topics such as relational aggression, depression, addiction in youth, and self-injury.